Shadows of his Coming

Wm. M. Juring

Published by

THE HOUSE OF WAYMARK

P.O. Box 13586
Roseville, Minnesota 55113

Library of Congress Cataloging - in - Publishing Data

Juring, Wm. M.
  Shadows of his Coming / Wm. M. Juring

ISBN 0-9634885-0-3

Published by The House of Waymark
P.O. Box 13586
Roseville, MN. 55113
Printed in the United States of America

Acknowledgments

When looking back over the years, I have come to realize God's blessing of special people in my life. Among them a loving wife and family without who's support this study would have had little chance of being completed.

It should also be mentioned this study would not have gotten started if the Lord had not introduced me to one of his own. A special friend, who with great patience and help encouraged me in the early hours of this endeavor.

For all your time and effort Mike, may the Lord richly bless you.

Contents

Shadows of his Coming

Introduction

Many believe the Church is living in the last days, that period referred to in Scripture as the time just before the return of Christ. If they are correct, would not the coming antichrist be alive as well?

Surprisingly, when recent world events are examined along with Scripture's prophetic warnings, there is considerable evidence that as the world's future tyrant, the antichrist is introduced during this period of time.

The basis for the question about the antichrist is twofold. First, Scripture has forewarned the Church that it is to "watch and pray" concerning certain world events that will usher in Christ's return. Secondly, and equally important, Scripture goes on to imply that beginning with Israel's rebirth as a nation, that chosen generation will witness Christ's second coming.

The problem here is that many have lost hold of the fact that the word "watch" is not just some idle or passive suggestion, but is instead a valid command requiring active and constant research by the Church. As a result of this negligence, many are lulled into believing there is nothing to fear at this time. Consequently, they are not able to recognize Scripture's prophetic warnings.

Briefly looking at some of the signs the Church has been commanded to be on guard for, the following may well prove to be a challenge for some within it. They begin with Revelation's prophecy about the destruction of the world's financial center. A city so powerful financially that her loss causes a catastrophic collapse to both business and banking communities throughout the world. And, according to Scripture, it is this city's destruction that brings the world's leaders together in search for a solution to this economic meltdown, members of a world government it describes as "the beast".

Following this financial disintegration, Scripture forewarns that the antichrist is now introduced. According to Scripture, he is both politically and militarily endowed, and because of his intense hatred for Israel, the most feared of man's carnage is unleashed -- Armageddon. A battle that the prophet Micah further suggests takes place within that generation of Israel's rebirth as a nation.

Despite the fact that the antichrist had not yet been introduced, the question of Armageddon became an issue for many during the 1990-91 Gulf War. And, although this confrontation appears to have been contained, their question still may be valid due to the fragile outcome of this military encounter.

This grim forecast is derived not only from the fact that Iraq is anti-Jewish, but that it was forced out of Kuwait by Israel's strongest supporter, the United States. A nation, who in its effort to undermine Iraq's hope of uniting the Arab world against Israel, spearheaded the successful UN coalition against Iraq. An embarrassment to Iraq that will not easily be overlooked, especially when one considers that along with this humiliation, Iraq was then allowed to retreat from Kuwait with its Revolution Command Council still intact and under Saddam Hussein's control.

As for the Gulf War and those who study end-time prophecy, most are aware that just before Christ's return, the Middle East is described as capturing the spotlight of world events. Yet few realize that Micah also prophecies that the antichrist comes from the area of modern day Iraq.

Along with the Scripture dealing with the coming financial problems, the following pages will examine references to two important issues regarding the beast government and the antichrist who eventually controls it. First, it comes to power from a collective world government system. And second, the most significant to this study, the throne or capital of this world government is in a city called "Mystery Babylon", a multifaceted city described in Scripture as the world's financial center of its day, before its destruction.

Regarding the identity of Mystery Babylon, countless generations have, without success, ventured to identify this city and the beast government of which it is associated. Among them were indictments and theories conceived with a great deal of conviction, even so, one significant fact was absent to support their findings. That missing element was

Israel becoming a nation for the second time, a component that Scripture reveals is paramount for the fulfillment of this city's sought after identity.

Dispelling many of the myths and superstitions concerning Mystery Babylon, the fourth and fifth chapters of Micah are now examined, two segments of Old Testament Scripture where the key to unlocking the identity of Mystery Babylon is found. In these chapters are not only Micah's comments involving this city and Israel's return to the map of nations, but her soon-to-follow invasion by the antichrist. Along with Micah's description of this critical period, the following pages will explore Daniel and Revelation to add insight to this timely subject.

Proposing that the appearance of the beast government and the antichrist may be much closer than many within the Church realizes, this study does not, in any manner, attempt to identify the day or the hour of Christ's return.

Chapter I

Micah, A Twentieth Century Prophet

Shadows of his Coming

In the following study of end-time prophecy, time and effort may prove to be well spent if one has ever questioned the Scripture's ability to accurately forecast the future.

Beginning with the book of Micah and his comments and admonitions about the last days, fulfilled prophecies become readily apparent as Micah's record confirms itself as God's instrument, and the twentieth century as the age for which it was written. A fact that becomes evident, even to one who has only a casual interest in prophecy.

As its author, Micah was born in the small town of Moresheth, 20 miles southwest of Jerusalem. There, as a Jewish child, he was raised in all the Jewish laws and culture some 800 years before the birth of Christ.

It was from this rural setting that the Lord called Micah as His oracle to the Jewish nation. Here Micah's opening chapters reveal that he not only advised Israel of their sin and disobedience, but he also predicted that one day God would turn His back on the Jewish nation as the price for their refusal to follow God's leading.

Despite Israel's warning of judgment, Micah's reprimand concludes with two encouraging promises in chapter four. They are the pledge of restoration for Israel as a sovereign state, and that the Messiah appears shortly thereafter. Events that not only mirrors the twentieth century, but the immediate years to follow.

Following the promise of the Messiah's reign in the opening verses of chapter four, Micah's outline changes in verse six as he reviews the years just before Israel's rebirth. Here Micah begins a description of pain and suffering the Jewish people must now endure, comparing their desire for statehood to a woman in childbirth.

Continuing in chapter four, verse 11 records Micah warning the Jewish people that after they become a new nation, hostile enemies will be invading her borders. These prove to be adversaries that Micah implies pave the way for the antichrist and his forces. And, according to verse 12, all are doomed to fail.

Except for the invasion of Israel by the antichrist and the promised reign of Israel's Messiah, a careful study of Micah's fourth chapter reveals that all of his prophecies have been fulfilled. Further, they all have taken place since the turn of the twentieth century. A journey of tears and near annihilation that began with the Zionist movement under Theodore Herzel in 1897.

As for the hardships they endured, most have proven to be a catalyst, instilling within the hearts of the Jewish people the resolve to defend themselves against any adversary threatening their survival as a nation. A test of perseverance that began in 1948 when six Arab states invaded Israel within hours of it becoming a nation.

As the following verses open this study, they begin with Micah summarizing ancient Israel's sin and perversion and God warning them of the coming judgment to Israel as a nation. A prophecy that became reality for the Jewish people beginning in 70 A.D.

Israel, A Condemned Nation

Micah: Chapter 3
Vs. 9
> Hear this, I pray you, ye heads of the house of Jacob, and princes of the house of Israel, that abhor justice, and pervert all equity.

Vs. 10
> They build up Zion with blood, and Jerusalem with iniquity.

Vs. 11
> Her heads [rulers] judge for reward, and her priests teach for hire, and her prophets divine for money; yet will they lean upon the Lord and say, is not God among us? No evil can come upon us.

15

Vs. 12

> Therefore shall Zion for your sake be
> plowed as a field, and Jerusalem shall
> become heaps, and the mountain of the
> Lord as the high places of the forests.

In this summary of Israel before the birth of
Christ, Micah boldly warns the Jewish people that
God has taken note of their corrupted morals. And
unless they repent, Micah adds that Israel will be
judged unworthy of remaining a nation. Micah also
indicts the religious leaders of that period stating
that they are only in the ministry for the revenue
it offers. An accusation he charges those in government as well, adding that the judgment of Israel is
due to their unwillingness to change their wicked
ways. And should this warning be defied, Micah
goes on to caution that the nation of Israel will become like some mountain wilderness, and her cities
piles of rock and ruble.

There are, however, words of hope attached to
this reprimand, as chapter four continues with a
unexpected promise:

Her Glorious Future

Micah: Chapter 4,
Vs. 1

> But in the last days it shall come to pass,
> that the mountain of the house of the
> Lord shall be [again] established in the
> top of the mountains, and it shall be

exalted above all the hills, and people shall flow unto it.

Vs. 2

And many nations shall come, and say, come, and let us go up to the mountain of the Lord, and to the house of the God of Jacob; and he will teach us of His ways, and we will walk in his paths; for the law shall go forth from Zion, and the word of the Lord from Jerusalem.

Vs. 3

And He shall judge among many peoples, and rebuke strong nations afar off; and they shall beat their swords into plow shares, and their spears into pruning-hooks; nation shall not lift up a sword against nation, neither shall they learn war anymore.

Vs. 4

But they shall sit every man under his vine and under his fig tree, and none shall make him afraid; for the mouth of the Lord of host has spoken it.

Within these verses, Micah records future events that the Church and the Jewish community have envisioned for two thousand years. This prophetic description not only includes the rebirth of Israel and the implied return of Christ, but Micah further states that Israel will go on to become the world's dominant power.

According to verse one, Micah's comment about the "**mountain**" likens Israel to the tallest peak of some distant mountain range, with the foothills surrounding it as to serve and guard her. So it will be for the future nation of Israel as it journeys to become an international power. A nation so influential, it leaves all the other governments of the world looking like only hills in comparison: "**In the top of the mountains** [or greatest of nations], **and it shall be above the hills.**"

These verses also contend that Israel will be walking in "**His** [Messiah's] **ways**" and that as the world's leading figure, "**He will judge among many people.**" The implication here is that by this time Christ has returned and has begun His earthly reign from the city of Jerusalem as Israel now becomes the focal point of the entire world.

The topic of war is also addressed in these verses as the military armament of the world is dismantled, with nations guilty of aggression judged accordingly. How different the world is pictured here as Micah records the nations converting their military assets toward peacetime endeavors. Tranquility and calm that confirm the Messiah's reign on earth is now established.

In verse five, however, a puzzling comment is made regarding spiritual interests during this time of political change:

Vs. 5

> **For all people will walk in the name of his god, but we will walk in the name of the Lord, our God, forever and ever.**
> (Amplified Version)

Although verse five is not perfectly clear, further study reveals it to be an indictment concerning the people living in the days just before Christ's return and their lack of identifying the importance of this prophetic time. This becomes evident as Micah adds here that there will exist at this time other "gods", idolatry that would hardly be tolerated after Christ's return.

Micah appears to be implying, that except for a select few who are looking for the prophetic signs and warnings leading up to this blessed event, the rest of the world will be preoccupied with other interests, not realizing the critical era in which they are a part.

Scripture supports this theory in the following verses as Micah goes on to detail world events that will identify this important prophecy:

The Returning Remnant

Vs. 6

In that day saith the Lord, will I assemble her that is lame, and I will gather her that is driven out, and her that I have afflicted;

Vs. 7

And I will make her that was lame a remnant, and her that was cast off a strong nation; and the Lord shall reign over them in Mount Zion from henceforth, even forever.

19

Beginning with verse six, Micah focuses on the Jewish people and that time in their history when God will be calling them back to the Holy Land. Opening with the comment: "**In that day**", Micah clearly associates this text's description of Israel's rebirth with that critical period of the Messiah's reign. Micah further confirms this connection with the comment that when God recalls the Jewish people, they are portrayed as have been previously "**cast off**" (or scattered about). The implication here is that at this prophetic time, the Jewish people are gathered from all corners of the world, from which will emerge the new nation of Israel.

In the following verse, Micah addresses a subject that has seldom been explored. It involves both Israel's rebirth and the generation that will usher her into statehood -- and how the two are both related to his prophecy of the Messiah's coming:

Vs. 8

> **And thou, O tower of the flock, the stronghold of the daughter of Zion -- <u>unto you shall it come</u> -- <u>even the first domin-ion</u> -- the kingdom shall come to the daughter of Jerusalem.**

When examined, this verse contains a promise to the Jewish people that deserves some careful review. With the comment: "**And thou, O tower of the flock,**" Micah quotes a term that shepherds use when one of their flock stands out above the others. He is implying that the generation living at the time of Israel's rebirth is very special. He

20

supports this statement by further stating that they will not only be living in that hour when Israel is again summoned to be a nation, but even more significant, many from this generation will be alive to witness Christ's return: **"Unto you shall it come -- even** [the glory of] **the first dominion** [of Israel]." This controversial subject will be examined in the following pages.

A People in Travail

Beginning in verse nine, Micah adds to this important prophecy by describing the days just before Israel becomes a nation again, comparing their efforts and frustrations to the labor pains of a woman about to give birth:

Vs. 9

Now why do you cry aloud? Is there no king in thee? Is thy counselor perished? For pangs have overtaken thee as a woman in travail.

Vs. 10

Be in pain, and labor to bring forth, O daughter of Zion, like a woman in travail; for now thou shalt go forth out of the city, and thou shalt dwell in the field, and thou shalt go to Babylon, there thou shalt be delivered; there the Lord shall redeem thee from the hand of thine enemies.

After pointing out their intense longings to be their own nation, with leaders supporting Jewish values and customs, Micah challenges the Jewish people forward in their quest for statehood by telling them to **"be in pain -- and labor to bring forth."** This goal, nonetheless, requires this chosen remnant to leave their homes and personal comforts in exchange for the barren settlements in the new Israel. **"For now thou shalt go forth out of the city -- and thou shalt dwell in the field."**

Micah also makes a confusing comment in verse ten. He contends here that Israel's statehood is in fact directly related to a location he labels as **"Babylon"**. According to this verse, it is in this assigned place that their future as a nation is determined. **"There thou shalt be delivered,"** as God now opens the door for Israel to become a nation for a second time.

Unfortunately, because verse ten lists the site of Israel's rebirth as Babylon, it has been interpreted by some as referring to Israel's captivity in 445 B.C. and as having nothing to do with the balance of this prophetic chapter. It should noted, however, that this is the only time in the Old Testament record where the name Babylon is used in a specific text where the author did not include either the name of a Babylonian king or some nearby nation to fully identify it. This is significant, not because this passage of Scripture proves that Micah is referring to a new or different Babylon, but because the Church cannot document from this text that Micah is referring to the original Babylon.

Micah's tenth verse then raises a question which deserves some serious study, one that in fact becomes the crux of this report: Is Scripture referring here to a different Babylon? A twentieth century community which according to Scripture, would be active in both the world's political and financial affairs -- while having an active roll in Israel's rebirth. This question will be better addressed in subsequent pages, for when all the facts are presented, Scripture will later verify verse ten's comment about Babylon as belonging to chapter four and a key verse within it.

The Birth of A Nation

Beginning with verse 11, Scripture focuses on Israel's first hours as a new nation, how she will be attacked by foreign armies, and on the aftermath of those that wish to annihilate her:

Vs. 11
Now also many nations are gathered against thee, that say, let her be defiled, and let our eye look upon Zion.

Vs. 12
But they know not the thoughts of the Lord, neither understand they His counsel, for He shall gather them as sheaves unto the floor.

Just as King Herod tried unsuccessfully to steal the hope of salvation from the Church by attempting to have Christ killed as a young child, so does

Micah warn Israel of impending danger in these two verses. He points out that immediately after Israel becomes a sovereign nation, hostile enemies will "**now**" rise in battle against her.

Here again Scripture is proven accurate, for within hours of the British surrendering Palestine (Israel) to the Jewish people and withdrawing from her shores, six fully armed Arab nations attacked her borders from all sides. They are adversaries, that paralleling verse 12, will not have discerned God's plan for the new nation of Israel. "**They know not the thoughts of the Lord, neither understand they his counsel,**" as Micah further describes how Israel's enemies are gathered as sheaves piled high on some threshing floor.

The military statistics of June 15, 1948, bear proof of Micah's prophetic accuracy, when with her limited and antiquated armament, Israel fulfilled Micah's prediction. On that prophesied day as it obtained statehood, the total of Israel's armed forces consisted of only nine substandard brigades. Their weapons included the small sum of 195 three-inch mortars, plus some old Hispano-Suiza 20MM cannons and some French 65MM Howitzers dating from the turn of the century. Besides being poorly equipped, their armored units consisted of only a few scout cars and some crudely fashioned armored vehicles, with very little radio contact between any of them.

With this inadequate armament, Israel successfully fought off six fully armed nations. Numbered among them were not only Egypt and the Saudi Arabian armies, but Iraq, Jordan, Lebanon and Syria as well. Included in this invasion were heavy air strikes from Iraq, Egypt and Syria, with the latter two countries employing tanks. Jordan, Lebanon and Iraq also added their armored car contingents. And all of their forces fully trained by European instructors, notably by the French and English during World War II.

But God had a plan for the new nation of Israel, one that includes both success and honor as He promises to stand behind them in victory:

Vs. 13

> **Arise and thresh, O daughter of Zion, I will make thine horn iron, and I will make thy hoofs bronze; and thou shalt beat in pieces many peoples; and I will consecrate their gain unto the Lord, and their substance unto the Lord of the whole earth.**

Israel is not only told here to defend herself. She is also given the promise that in her future, the Lord will make her into a first-class military power: "**And I will make thy horn iron and thy hoofs bronze.**" This comment regarding Israel's horn of iron and hoofs of bronze suggests an elite army of both strength and grandeur, proving to the world that God is doing something very special within the new nation of Israel.

Looking back at Israel's stunning exploits covering that period between 1948 and the present, Israel has for the most part amazed the world, including her enemies. She has also proven herself a formidable opponent to any nation considering going to war against her. History reveals these

clashes began with Egypt nationalizing the Suez
Canal in 1956, an ill-fated move by Egypt designed
to strip Israel's access to this important waterway.
Israel's next battle was the six-day war in 1967, a
brilliant and decisive campaign that allowed Israel
to regain control of Jerusalem and the Temple site.

In addition to these victories is the "Yom
Kippur War" of 1973 against the three nations of
Egypt, Syria and Jordan, and the removal of the
PLO from Lebanon in 1982. And, further supporting verse 13 and its promise of victory for Israel,
are the many raids, air strikes and artillery ex-
changes throughout the intervening years.

It should be noted that even though Micah's
fourth chapter concludes with verse 13, the subject
of Israel's rebirth and her succeeding hours are
continued in the following chapter. Consequently,
the opening verses of chapter five will be examined
at this time as they contain a critical element regarding Israel's rebirth. When examined, however,
these verses describe two different topics from two
distinct periods of Israel's history, both of which
relate to her becoming a nation again.

The Coming Siege

Micah: Chapter 5
Vs. 1a

> **Now gather thyself in troops, O daughter**
> **of troops -- he [the coming antichrist] has**
> **laid siege against us --**

When correctly placed, this opening comment about Israel's coming invasion, should be instead, the closing statement of Micah's fourth chapter.

This segment of verse one is a warning to Israel of a great military event, an invasion that takes place shortly after Israel becomes a nation. And when included as part of the previous verses, it then completes the long chain of events concerning Israel's struggle for survival with the introduction of the antichrist. Several facts within this verse support this claim, beginning with Micah's referring to them once again as **"daughters"** as in the previous eighth verse.

The word **"now"** also appears here again in verse one (1a), and in so doing, Micah ties this statement to that pivotal period when Israel would be a new nation -- and to Christ's return.

In addition, the reference to **"us"** in verse one is plural and is directed toward the Jewish people. According to the opening comment of verse one, they are to put aside their personal differences and be as united as possible because **"he"**, the coming antichrist, now makes his move against Israel at this time.

In summary, Micah is warning the Jewish people, that shortly after they become a nation for the second time, a military invasion will take place. It will be an encounter against Israel that sets the stage for the Battle of Armageddon as, **"he has laid siege against us."**

Past Sin, Judgment and Pardon

In the second half of verse one, Micah introduces a new theme as he outlines in reversed sequence the primary cause why the Jewish people lived the past 19 centuries without having a nation of their own. And although it touches on a new subject, it does pertain to this important matter of Israel's rebirth:

Vs. 1b
-- They shall smite the judge of Israel with a rod upon the cheek.

Vs. 2
But thou, Bethlehem Ephratah, though thou be little among the thousands of Judah, out of thee shall he come forth unto me who is to be ruler in Israel, whose goings forth have been of old, from everlasting.

Beginning in the second half of verse one, Micah calls attention to Israel's rejection of their Messiah by the Jewish leaders. However, Micah's message is presented in a reversed sequence. Micah begins by proclaiming: **"They shall smite the judge of Israel with a rod."** This statement is then followed in verse two with the added promise that **"Bethlehem"** will be the birthplace of Israel's coming judge and king. **"Out of thee shall he** [the Messiah] **come forth."**

In this inverted prophecy, Micah not only predicts about the city involving Christ's birth, but also of Israel's rejection of Him as the promised Messiah. Micah then adds that Christ's rejection is the principal reason for God dismantling the first nation of Israel. It is a reprimand that has limitations, however, as the following verse explains:

Vs. 3
Therefore will He give them up -- until the time that she which travaileth has brought forth; then the remnant of his brethren shall return unto the children of Israel.

Although not readily apparent, the opening three verses of chapter five are critical to this study. They not only reveal the reasons God terminated the nation of Israel as a sovereign territory, but verse three confirms that Micah's previous tenth verse belonged to this critical event of Israel's rebirth. This assertion is supported in the comment **"Therefore will He give them up, until the time that she** [the Jewish people] **which travaileth has brought forth."** A statement that points directly to verse ten and Micah's statement **"Be in pain and labor to bring forth."**
It should be noted again that it was in the previous tenth verse that Micah prophesied to the Jewish people **"you will go to Babylon, there you will be delivered."** Of interest here is the fact that this prophetic statement clearly suggests that in the last days, an evil and corrupt site would

have a major role in allowing Israel to be again established as a nation.

Summary: Micah Chapter Four

Along with Scripture's comments about the antichrist, one of the goals of this study is to challenge Micah's mysterious reference to a city critical to Israel's rebirth, a location he called "**Babylon**". It is essential, therefore, to depart temporarily from Micah's record and explore other Scripture for the needed background before examining his concluding remarks. The basis for such an inquiry are Micah's comment about the pain and suffering that would proceed Israel's rebirth, and his alluding to these events as belonging to "**that day**" in which the Messiah will appear. For within Micah's simple, yet powerful indictment, one must face the fact that the twentieth century may be that pivotal period about which this prophecy is given.

Looking back into the first half of the twentieth century and the years just before it, the prophetic accuracy of Micah's fourth chapter becomes increasingly evident. But to grasp its full significance, the life of Theodore Herzel (1860-1904), the father of modern-day Israel should also be briefly examined.

In 1897, Herzel founded The World Zionist Organization. It would be a movement designed not only to awaken Jewish consciousness in Judaism and its Hebrew language, but it also included Jewish literature, the arts, and even more significant, stimulating the Jewish people's will to rebuild a Jewish state in the land of Palestine.

It was shortly after these seeds of pride and nationalism were sown and taking root, that the Jewish people were forced to endure their worst hours. Europe was to be torn apart by Adolph Hitler with his commission from hell to destroy not only Jewish lives, but their dream of a new Israel (1938-45). History records this period as the Holocaust. A time of anguish from which would emerge a generation committed to becoming a nation again.

Had Micah's portrayal of the Jewish people as a homeless and rejected remnant been in error, or had Israel's enemies stopped them from becoming the nation she has come to be, attempts to identify current-day Israel with Micah's fourth chapter would be difficult.

Recent history, nonetheless, has proven these prophecies to be accurate. And, should one accept the premise that Micah's fourth chapter refers to another time, a brief study of Isaiah's chapter 11 would be appropriate at this time.

In this chapter, Isaiah begins by describing the peace that the world will experience when the Messiah will have claimed His rightful dominion over the earth. But in verse 11, Isaiah's prophecy focuses on the time just before the Messiah's coming with a critical announcement:

Vs. 11a

> And it shall come to pass in that day [at that time], **that the Lord shall set his hand again -- <u>the second time</u> -- to recover the remnant of his people who shall be left ...**

When Isaiah's comments are closely examined, it is evident that there will be a second "recovery" for the Jewish people and that it will be near the time of Christ's return. It is also safe to assume that this text is referring to the two birth periods that Israel would have as a nation. Scripture records the first recovery when Moses lead their exodus from Egypt fifteen hundred years before Christ. History records the second beginning on May 14, 1948.

With the similarity established between Micah's Old Testament record and the present nation of Israel, the question concerning the location of Israel's rebirth and the possible reason for Micah referring to it as "Babylon" must now be addressed. However, this becomes a controversial topic because history records the city of New York as the actual site involved with Israel becoming a nation again. In this prominent city, the UN General Assembly voted 33 to 13 to allow the Jewish people to once again occupy the Hold Land. And as a result of this UN decision, New York became the city responsible for fulfilling Micah's prophecy.

This subject of Micah's Babylon and its connection to the city of New York, is further addressed in the following study of Revelation 18.

Chapter II

"Mystery Babylon" Could It Be?

Shadows of his Coming

As we continue to explore Micah's prophecy about a site called Babylon, its involvement with Israel's rebirth, and their connection with the city of New York, the following pages will examine the book of Revelation and its comments regarding a city it also calls Babylon.

The name Babylon as used in this text is symbolic, referring to its predecessor of the past. A community noted for its wealth, luxury and unrestrained wickedness. Founded by Nimrod, the great-grandson of Noah in 2100 B.C., Babylon was destroyed by the Medes some fifteen hundred years later in 538 B.C.

According to Scripture, Mystery Babylon is a city that will not be easily identified, at least not at the time of its introduction. This fact is made evident with Revelation's addition of the word "mystery" to the city's title. A word implying that its location will not be fully known without a period of waiting and an in-depth search of the Scriptures.

Studies on this subject, however, have proven it to be both a difficult and confusing topic. This is due not only to the fact that its prophecy is often given by more than one prophet or messenger, but that their prophecies are not always arranged in the order in which they will occur.

Therefore, to better recognize Revelation's evidence concerning this city's identity, the following two chapters will be examined in reverse order, beginning with chapter 18 and then going back to chapter 17. The reversed chapters will better describe a city with world-wide financial influence and great political power just before Christ's return. And, according to Revelation, it will be Mystery Babylon's destruction that causes the downfall of the world's monetary system, devastation that is described by the Apostle John in the following verses:

The Church is Warned

Revelation: Chapter 18
Vs. 1
And after these things I saw another angel come down from heaven, having great power; and the earth was lightened with his glory.

Vs. 2
And he cried with a mighty voice, saying, Babylon the great is fallen, is fallen, and is become the habitation of devils, and the

hold of every foul spirit, and a cage of
every unclean and hateful bird.

Vs. 3
For all the nations have drunk of the wine
of the wrath of her fornication, and the
kings of the earth have committed fornication with her, and the merchants of the
earth are grown rich through the abun-
dance of her delicacies.

After receiving several previous visions, John
opens this chapter recording another revelation. In
this new encounter, details are given about Mystery
Babylon, beginning with an angel describing its
immoral condition. But before John records any of
the angel's comments, he notes that the world was
made bright with the angel's arrival. It is a comment suggesting that in the last days, the Church
would no longer be in the dark about this city's
true identity.

John then implies that the angel awakens the
Church to this concealed truth with a loud and
powerful voice, calling attention to the fact that
Mystery Babylon has **"fallen"**.

The term "fallen" as used in this text, refers to
a slow descent, like a bird when landing or like a
leaf when dropping from a tree as both float slowly
to the ground. Consequently, the angel in this text
is not describing some war or earthquake, or any
other physical destruction or collapse. He is instead
referring to a city that was once moral and God-
fearing, but is now living in sin, one that according
to this text **"has become the home of devils and**

every foul spirit." Scripture then confirms the fact that as a city it has slipped into an immoral condition, as it compares it to a cage filled with **"every unclean and hateful bird."**

Adding further to this indictment is verse three's comment that the nations of the world become infected with this city's sinful lifestyle, including business communities, heads of state and national leaders. Scripture implies here that as a city it has squandered its great wealth and energy on a decadent way of life; one that the world has not only witnessed, but also emulates.

It is apparent that Scripture is describing this city as one that has failed God and is deserving of judgment as the following verses now affirms:

A City is Judged

Vs. 4

And I heard another voice from heaven, saying, come out of her my people, that you be not partakers of her sins, and that you receive not of her plagues.

Vs. 5

For her sins have reached unto heaven, and God has remembered her iniquities.

Beginning with verse four, another voice is heard as it cautions the Church with a warning similar to the one given Lot and his family recorded in Genesis 19. With the command: **"Come out**

of her my people," it clearly alerts the Church living in Mystery Babylon to leave before it takes on her godless way of life -- and judgment.

Supporting this assertion are the following Scripture verses as they now reveal details about Mystery Babylon's judgment:

Vs. 6

Reward her even as she rewarded you, and double unto her double according unto her works; in the cup that she has filled, fill to her double.

Vs. 7

How much she has glorified herself, and lived luxuriously, so much torment and sorrow give her; she has said in her heart, "I sit as a queen, and am no widow, and I shall see no sorrow."

Vs. 8

Therefore shall her plaques come in one day, death, and mourning, and famine, and she shall be utterly burned with fire; for strong is the Lord God who judgeth her.

According to verse six, when Mystery Babylon is judged, it will be double in proportion to the city's sin and wickedness. The comment about the cup in this verse is tied directly to a statement examined later in Revelation 17:4. In this verse, Scripture will portray this cup as a golden goblet overflowing with sin and corruption. And even more interesting is the fact that as a city, Mystery Babylon will be arrogantly holding this cup of sin out in full view for all the world to witness.

Having little doubt or question about the city's prominent status, Mystery Babylon is also described as being proud and boastful. According to this text, it is a city that mistakenly believes it will never experience hardship or tragedy, for **"I sit as a queen** [and] **I shall see no sorrow."**

In verse eight, Scripture adds a serious comment regarding the intense destruction of Mystery Babylon. Recording the word **"plague"** it implies here that many of this city's population will be stricken by the hand of God. Supporting this claim, Scripture inserts that the city's judgment will entail death, famine and destruction by fire.

Scripture's mention of Mystery Babylon's burning is difficult to imagine, especially now that cities are subject to strict fire code requirements. Yet, with all these restrictive measures, this great city is destroyed within **"one day"**.

A Stunned World

In the following verses, John records comments from the world's leaders following the destruction of Mystery Babylon:

Vs. 9

And the kings of the earth, who have committed fornication and lived luxuriously with her, shall bewail her, and lament for

**her, when they shall see the smoke of her
burning.**

Vs. 10
**Standing afar off for the fear of her tor-
ment, saying, alas, alas, that great city,
Babylon, that mighty city! For in one hour
is thy judgment come.**

As Scripture continues with its charges against
Mystery Babylon, it prophecies how the world's
political community will respond when this city is
destroyed.

Noting **"the fear of her torment,"** verse ten
describes the severity of this city's destruction and
its devastating impact to the world. And, in a comment that could only mean one thing in this age of
nuclear annihilation, it condenses the time frame of
Mystery Babylon's destruction from "one day" to
"one hour".

It is also apparent by these verses, that its
destruction affects not only the commerce within its
own nation, but also that of other economies as
Scripture adds that the merchants of the earth,
watching it burn from afar, weep in disbelief:

Vs. 11
**And the merchants of the earth shall weep
and mourn over her; for no man buyeth
their merchandise any more.**

With the world facing financial collapse, Scripture reveals how the business community, which
previously depended on this city's existence for

39

their success, is stunned to their financial core at the report of this city's destruction. This leaves the question of just how influential is this city within the world's business community. This question is answered beginning with verse 12 as Scripture launches a detailed description of this city:

The Empty Marketplace

Vs. 12

> The merchandise of gold, and silver -- and precious stones, and pearls -- and fine linen, and purple, and silk, and scarlet -- and all thyine wood, and all kinds of ivory vessels, and all kinds of vessels of precious woods, and of bronze, and iron, and marble.

First on Revelation's list is **"gold and silver"**, which represents not only the metals themselves, but also the banking industry which has helped this city to become world renowned. The **"fine linen, purple, silk and scarlet"** refer to the garment industry, which would also include the fashion designers for which this city would be noted.

Scripture's mention of **"thyine** [or costly] **wood"**, refers to the accessory items found in most home and commercial decorating studios, as well as the **"ivory vessels, bronze, iron and marble"** which this city is world famous. This list is far from over as the following verses continue to point to only one major city:

40

Vs. 13

And cinnamon, and odors, and ointments, and frankincense -- and wine, and oil, and fine flour, and wheat, and cattle, and sheep -- and horses, and chariots -- and slaves, and the souls of men.

Vs. 14

And the fruits that thy soul lusted after are departed from thee, and all things which were dainty and sumptuous are departed from thee, and thou shalt find them no more at all.

Vs. 15

The merchants of these things who where made rich by her, shall stand afar off for the fear of her torment, weeping and wailing.

Vs. 16

And saying, alas, alas, that great city, that was clothed in fine linen, and purple, and scarlet, covered with gold, and precious stones, and pearls!

As these verses add their testimony to Mystery Babylon's identification, they begin by including **"cinnamon, odors, ointments and frankincense."** These ingredients refer to the cosmetic industry, and like the previous clues, all point to New York City.

The **"wine, oil, fine flour, cattle and sheep"** comprise the food commodities of which New York

41

is not only one of the world's largest brokers, but a consumer as well. **"Horses and chariots"** are one unit and refer to its air and land capabilities for moving people, with **"slaves and the souls of men"** on this list possibly representing the prostitution and drug trades for which this famous city is noteworthy. Again, New York is a world leader in both areas.

Within these few verses, Scripture not only describes the details of this city's destruction, but also the extent of its loss to the world's retail markets. Verse 16 then records the merchant's comments as they describe this city in terms of royal apparel. **"Clothed in fine linen, and purple, and scarlet, covered with gold, and precious stones, and pearls."**

Scripture continues to gives additional insight about this city's identity as the following text describes one of its important borders:

Vs. 17

> **For in one hour so great riches are come to nothing. And every shipmaster, and all the company in ships, and sailors, and as many as trade by the sea, stood afar off.**

Not only does Scripture mention here for the second time that Mystery Babylon will be destroyed within the brief period of "one hour", but it reinforces the theory for it being New York City, recording here that it is a port city on international waters. And as such, it is visited by seagoing vessels from various nations, **"as many as trade by the sea."** Merchant seaman, who because of the severity of this city's destruction, must stand **"afar off."** And then being moved to tears after witnessing its destruction from their ships, they ask themselves: "What other city is like it?"

Vs. 18

> **And cried when they saw the smoke of her burning, saying, what city is like unto this city.**

Vs. 19

> **And they cast dust on their heads, and cried, weeping and wailing, saying, alas, alas, that great city, wherein were made rich all that had ships in the sea by reason of her costliness! For in one hour is she made desolate.**

As these verses confirm Mystery Babylon's destruction, it is obvious that it is a major trading center to the world's marketplace, her annihilation causes a severe shock to the world's financial community. Moreover, Scripture warns the Church here for the third time about this city's total destruction and that it will be destroyed in "one hour". The subject of Mystery Babylon's identity and destruction is continued in the following verses as Scripture now instructs the Church to rejoice over her judgment:

The Avenged Church

Vs. 20

> Rejoice over her, thou heaven, and you holy apostles and prophets; for God has avenged you on her.

Vs. 21

> And a mighty angel took up a stone like a great millstone, and cast it into the sea, saying, thus with violence shall that great city, Babylon, be thrown down, and shall be found no more at all.

At first glance, verse 20 gives the impression that Mystery Babylon is somehow directly involved with past sufferings within the Church. In fact, verse 24 of this study chapter will shortly verify that God is using this city as a symbol to represent all the communities of the past that refused to honor Him.

Scripture then goes on to underscore the destruction of Mystery Babylon as it describes an angel with a giant millstone, which with one thrust, casts the stone into the open sea. This illustration confirms the total and instant judgment coming to this city because it takes only a moment for the millstone to sink into the water and out of sight.

Continuing with Scripture's description of commercial Babylon, the following verses add to the supposition that New York City may indeed be this mystery city:

Vs. 22

> And the voice of harpers, and musicians, and flute players, and trumpeters, shall be heard no more at all in thee; and no craftsman, of any craft shall be found any more in thee, and the sound of a millstone shall be heard no more at all in thee.

Vs. 23

> And the light of a lamp shall shine no more at all in thee; and the voice of the bridegroom and the bride shall be heard no more at all in thee; for thy merchants were the great men of the earth; for by thy sorceries were all nations deceived.

Scripture points out here that Mystery Babylon is noted not only for its music and culture, but also for its skilled trades, expert craftsmen and general labor. And with the bride and groom as symbols of the future, Scripture adds that this city will never again see their joy as this city's lamp is darkened forever.

Adding to Mystery Babylon's identity is a new clue in verse 23. According to this text, the retail merchants of this city will have distinguished themselves by motivating the entire world with their clever ads and promotions, calling them the greatest on earth: **"For thy merchants were the great men of the earth for by they sorceries were all nations deceived."** This comment is very incriminating, especially when one considers the immense power and worldwide influence found in New York City's advertising and promotional firms.

45

As Revelation 18 concludes, it again comments about Mystery Babylon's sin and the seriousness of it:

Vs. 24
And in her was found the blood of prophets, and of saints, and of all that was slain upon the earth.

Difficult as it is to imagine, Scripture states here that **"The blood of all the prophets and saints, and of all that was slain upon the earth"**, from the beginning of time will be found in this evil city. This assertion does not mean to imply or even suggest that Mystery Babylon is personally responsible for generations of suffering and deaths to both saved and unsaved alike; rather it implies that the corrupt conditions that caused their anguish and torment appear again in this city's evil lifestyle -- conditions that have been ignored for the most part by its voters, courts and many of its churches.

Despite this chapter's prophetic outline, should one still question the probability that Mystery Babylon is a part of the United States, the following pages corroborate that New York City is at this time, the world's foremost candidate to be this mystery city.

Summary: Revelation Chapter 18

Throughout the history of the New Testament Church, Mystery Babylon has been compared to every major city since the time of Christ. Yet, at no other time in history has its description been more relevant than it is today, nor has there ever been a time in the last two thousand years when so many facts pointed to just one major city, New York.

An example of this incriminating evidence is Revelation's comment about the "horse and chariot". As earlier noted, this remark is in reference to Mystery Babylon's ability to move and transport people from one point to another. In the New York City subway system, there is over 700 miles of underground tracks, and in its five boroughs, 11,787 licensed taxicabs serving its commuting public (1992 figures). This is in addition to this city's three airports, who with their combined flights make New York City's air traffic controllers the busiest in the world.

As for the balance of Revelation's description of Mystery Babylon, the following is a list of the major similarities between it and those of New York City as described in chapter 18:

47

New York City
or
Mystery Babylon?

- ▶ Once godly, but is now demon-possessed.
  [verse 2]

- ▶ Christians living within its borders.
  [verse 4]

- ▶ Believes it is indestructible.
  [verse 7]

- ▶ Visited by world leaders and diplomats.
  [verse 9]

- ▶ Has influence on the world's economy.
  [verses 3, 11, and 15]

- ▶ Noted for banking and costly metals.
  [verse 12]

- ▶ Noted in the world's jewelry market.
  [verse 12]

- ▶ Leader in the garment/fashion industry.
  [verse 12]

- ▶ Has influence in the decorating fields.
  [verse 12]

▶ Leader in cosmetics and beauty aids.
[verse 13]

▶ A leader in the agricultural markets.
[verse 13]

▶ World leader in transportation.
[verse 13]

▶ Noted for prostitution/drug slavery.
[verse 13]

▶ World's wealthiest city.
[verse 16]

▶ A city with no equal or rival.
[verse 18]

▶ A seaport city open to world shipping.
[verses 17 and 19]

▶ A city of culture.
[verse 22]

▶ Noted for its clever merchandising.
[verse 23]

The following chart compares some of these mentioned characteristics to other famous cities along with New York. While all major cities have a certain degree of activity in the related areas of commerce, few are as prominent as the city of New York.

Noted Cities Of The Twentieth Century

	Tokyo	Paris	Rome	London	NYC
A PORT CITY					◆
BANKING/GOLD/SILVER	◆			◆	◆
JEWELRY		◆	◆		◆
SLAVERY=drugs/prostitution					◆
TRANSPORTATION	◆			◆	◆
ADVERTISING	◆			◆	◆
DECORATING		◆	◆		◆
WORLD'S WEALTHIEST CITY					◆

To many, the only convincing argument that New York City might be Mystery Babylon would be the witness of its destruction in the one hour or less as prophesied by Scripture. On the other hand, to one who takes Scripture seriously, and has not closed his or her eyes to the immoral conditions that persist almost arrogantly in the United States, the probability of Mystery Babylon being a part of this nation's culture is neither surprising nor totally remote.

Assuming then that New York City is in fact Mystery Babylon, two important questions remain: Who or what is Scripture referring to regarding this city's affiliation with the so-called beast? And, can that beast be verified as an integral part of New York City as Scripture implies?

These questions will be examined in the following pages as this study proceeds into the seventeenth chapter of Revelation.

Chapter III

The Beast of The Last Days

Shadows of his Coming

In Revelation 18, Scripture revealed a commercial (and geographical) portrait of Mystery Babylon. Beginning with the seventeenth chapter of Revelation, additional facts relating to this city's identity are now explored, including Scripture's mention of the "beast", its political structure and its strong affiliation with this city.

Throughout history, countless explanations of the so-called beast have been offered for consideration. Among the many are its references to a church, the rise of a second Roman Empire, and the European Common Market. In the upcoming pages concerning this subject, however, Scripture will prove these theories lack legitimate support.

Keeping in mind that all Scripture was written with a divine purpose, including its description of Mystery Babylon and the beast identified as part of this city, the following pages will explore the bond these two controversial subjects have with each other. And, when the two are examined side by side, they will prove to be an essential tool in identifying this end-time city for the Twentieth Century Church.

Believing that the angel's warning in Revelation 18 is written for the twentieth century, this study will now compare events recorded in Revelation 17 with recent history:

Revelation: Chapter 17
Vs. 1

And there came one of the seven angels who had the seven bowls, and talked with me, saying unto me, come here; I will show unto you the judgment of the great harlot that sitteth upon many waters;

Vs. 2

With whom the kings of the earth have committed fornication, and the inhabitants of the earth have been made drunk with the wine of her fornication.

Chapter 17 begins here with an angel offering to show John the judgment of a harlot described as sitting upon many waters. It should be noted that the "**harlot**" is only a symbol as is the "**many waters**". And according to verse 15 of this study chapter, the first represents the city it calls Mystery Babylon, with the waters the harlot is sitting on referring to a multilingual and densely populated area, where Scripture refers to them as "**peoples, multitudes, nations and languages.**"

The reasons for Scripture using the prostitute as the hallmark for Mystery Babylon will, when examined, prove obvious. Throughout history, a harlot is generally one who has little or no spiritual interest, and with little exception, becomes intimate with anyone for a price. So also is this great city whose last days John is to be shown. He is told in verse two that in the last days, she offers a relationship to the world and its leaders that will encourage them to become preoccupied with her self-centered way of life -- for a price.

The Scarlet-Colored Beast

Vs. 3

> **So he carried me away in the spirit into the wilderness and I saw a woman sit upon a scarlet colored beast, full of names of blasphemy, having seven heads and ten horns.**

Beginning with verse three, John is shown symbolic details of Mystery Babylon as Scripture records that he was lifted up by the angel and carried away in the spirit, **"into the wilderness."** In many modern Bible translations this term has been replaced with the word "desert". The reason for this change is not perfectly clear, except that in the original text, this word implies either a lonely or empty wasteland, a large territory -- or a desert.

Other than being a spiritual wasteland, the previous study of Revelation 18 discounted the desert theory, exposing the fact that Mystery Babylon is a port city on international waters and fully accessible to world shipping. If the word "desert" is a valid translation, one must then look for a seacoast city surrounded by sand, a geographical marvel which has never existed up to this point in time.

Building on the word "wilderness", however, a new possibility appears. The site or vicinity where the angel took John could in fact have been a land not yet established or developed, a location where this great and evil city would one day be erected.

Another comment deserving examination is John's statement: **"and I saw a woman sit upon a scarlet colored beast."** The word **"sit"** or sitting in this text implies that the woman is just resting upon or riding on an object. It is a description befitting a passenger along for the ride or journey, but not necessarily having any administrative control over the its destiny.

In addition, when the term **"beast"** is examined, Scripture suggests two interpretations: the first is a person or diplomat representing a government body, the other is the government itself. This is verified in Daniel's seventh chapter where he also addresses this subject in verse 12: **"As for the rest of the beasts** [members within the beast government], **they had their dominions** [or authority] **taken away, yet their lives were prolonged for a season and a time."** (Daniel's comments about the beast government are examined in the succeeding chapters.)

As for the beast in verse three, it will later be described as the controlling body of a global kingdom, one that has its headquarters in this world-class city represented by the harlot. A good example of such an arrangement would be London, as host city for England's Parliament and governing assembly, it has little or no special powers in the affairs of England's government.

The situation regarding New York City is very similar to London as it also enjoys both fame and revenue as host city to the United Nations. And, like the City of London and that of England's Parliament, New York has no special control over UN functions or its policies concerning the world and its problems.

Continuing with verse three's comments about the beast government being **"scarlet"** in color, and **"full of names of blasphemy"** (anti-God in structure), a fitting definition would be the remark found in Isaiah 1:18, "your sins are as scarlet." This indictment of blasphemy could easily point to the UN which, in its self-serving interests for fear of offending its membership, deliberately made no mention of God in its many charters.

In addition to not recognizing God as its source for strength and wisdom, the UN, as a global organization, has included in its membership, not only the democratic nations of the free world, but the socialist and powerful oil-rich Moslem countries of the Middle East as well, many of whom express open opposition to Judeo-Christian doctrine.

John also addressed the inner structure or composition of the beast in verse three, adding that it has **"seven heads and ten horns."** This statement is not describing some animal or creature from a horror movie. It is instead referring to a unique government controlled by a committee of seven special men, with ten additional members supporting them. The phrase "horns" also suggests that they have some degree of military involvement. Scripture will be covering both the seven heads and ten horns in more detail in a later portion of this chapter.

In verse four, the theme changes by calling attention to the spiritual condition of this world famous city as Scripture likens it to a "Harlot":

A Lady of The Night

Vs. 4

> **And the woman was arrayed in purple and scarlet color, and covered with gold and precious stones and pearls, having a golden cup in her hand, full of abominations and filthiness of her fornication.**

Described in the apparel of a prostitute, Mystery Babylon is pictured in verse four, dressed in her finest apparel, with scarlet and purple being the dress code of such in John's day. She is also covered with gold and precious jewels, giving her the added status of success in her trade. Interestingly, the golden goblet she holds is full of abominations. It is the portrait of a city that is not ashamed of her lifestyle, as she arrogantly displays it for all the world to see.

With all her sin out in plain view, Mystery Babylon becomes the forerunner, or **"mother"** of a godless approach to life, one that becomes very prominent in her day:

Vs. 5

And upon her forehead was a name writ-
ten, "MYSTERY, [or I am the mystery city]
BABYLON THE GREAT, THE MOTHER OF
HARLOTS AND ABOMINATIONS OF THE
EARTH."

Although given the name "Mystery" Babylon, the
true identity of this city will be obvious to both the
Church and those outside of it at some appointed
hour. This will only occur, however, when all the
commercial, geographical and political outlines
described both here in chapter 17 and in the
previous study chapter are met. At that time her
identification will be as though her name was
written "**upon her forehead**", out in full view for
the entire world to see.

Vs. 6

And I saw the woman drunk with the
blood of the saints, and with the blood of
the martyrs of Jesus; and when I saw her
I wondered with great admiration.

Verse Six appears to add to the record that
Mystery Babylon is someh'ow responsible for the
deaths of martyred saints: "**And I saw the woman
drunk with the blood of the saints.**" When fully
examined, however, a different picture begins to
unfold. This is primarily because verse six makes
no mention of the woman having any blood on her
hands, noting instead John's comment: "**and when
I saw her I wondered with great admiration.**"

The question remains; why is John admiring this evil city, when instead, one would think he would be horrified at it? In the original text, the word "admiration" implies that of: "great wonder, or to marvel at."

This query may be better answered by looking briefly again at Revelation 18:24 where it stated: **"in her** [Mystery Babylon] **was found the blood -- of all the saints -- slain upon the earth."**

Again, it is very unlikely that this city is guilty of any direct bloodshed regarding the Church, especially to the extent that it would be responsible for all the persecution and death **"of all the saints slain upon the earth."** It is possible, however, that John "marveled" because of this city's disregard for the pain and suffering of past saints who, from the beginning of time, were martyred because of the sin this city represents. Among its shortcomings would be pride, greed and sexual misconduct, just to name a few of its many failures. And the picture of her being drunk is also symbolic and refers to the serious extent of her sin. A city that is intoxicated on its perverted lifestyle while at the same time, being unaffected by God or anyone holding His values.

The real message in both Revelation 18:24, and verse six of this chapter is that Mystery Babylon will be destroyed as retribution for all the cities in which prophets and martyrs were killed.

A Mystery Revealed

In the following verses John elaborates on his vision as the angel verifies what some of its symbols imply:

Vs. 7
And the angel said to me, why do you wonder? I will tell you the mystery of the woman, and of the beast that carries her, which has the seven heads and the ten horns.

Vs. 8
The beast that you saw was and is not and shall ascend out of the bottomless pit and go into perdition; and they that dwell on the earth shall wonder, whose names are not written in the book of life from the foundation of the world, when they behold the beast that was -- and is not -- and yet is [to come].

This strange and curious statement about **"The beast that was -- and is not -- and yet is** [or will rise again]" has for centuries left the Church unsure as to the real message in this important declaration, even though it becomes self-explanatory when looking at it from John's perspective. When this verse is examined from that period of history when he recorded this encounter (70-90 A.D.), the angel's comment **"behold the beast that was"** would then imply that the beast government of the last days is actually some kind of carry-over from history. According to this verse, it is a type of government that would have had to exist before John and the New Testament Church.

The added comment that it **"is not"** would then suggest that this type of government was not active when John received his vision. This statement gives the Church an important clue about the government of the last days.

It is well-documented that John was exiled to the isle of Patmos by the Roman rulers in the First Century. The angel may be telling the Church in verse eight that the beast government will have nothing to do with -- or that it **"is not"** -- the Roman government of John's confinement.

Scripture also embellishes the facts regarding this mystery government in power upon Christ's return, pointing out that the unsaved from **"the foundation of the world"** will be surprised when they behold the author of it. It would be prudent then to look into history relevant to the Apostle John at the time of his exile.

Interestingly, ancient Greek history may hold the secret toward which Scripture is pointing. It was in Greek culture five centuries before Christ (and John) that the parliamentary process of democracy was born. The idea of a government made up of a collection of smaller governments in which the citizenry or their representatives hold the ruling power sounds very upright and innocent; however, the idea of a government built on the principles of self-rule does not align itself with Scripture, especially when it abandons God's word as a basis for its direction. This fact supports verse eight's implied comment that the lost of the world will have their eye's opened when, in hell, they see its origin.

In addition to Scripture's reference that the beast government could be parliamentary in design, the following verses confirm the fact that this government is formed from a coalition of 17 men representing 17 nations. Verse nine begins, however, cautioning on the need for wisdom in the interpretation of seven of its members:

Vs. 9

And here is the mind which hath wisdom, the seven heads are seven mountains, on which the woman sitteth.

Here again some confusion exists. In many Bible translations the word **"mountains"** recorded in this text reads as "hills". As a result, verse nine has led many to assume that the ancient city of Rome is Mystery Babylon because it also is constructed on seven hills. To better understand the real meaning of this verse; it should be examined along with Revelation 13:3. In this text it discusses this same subject but adds that one of these same seven heads receives a deadly wound.

Should one accepts the heads in verse nine as representing the seven hills under the city of Rome, the question then remains, how could a "hill" receive a deadly wound? The correct term should read "seven mountains", and refers to the seven nations that form the core, or foundation of this government called the beast with which Mystery

Babylon is associated. This subject of the heads is examined in a later portion of this study as the following text now focuses on the fact that there is an additional list of eight important kingdoms which must also be carefully considered at this time.

Eight Special Kingdoms

Vs. 10

> **And -- there are seven kings, five are fallen, and one is, and the other has not yet come; and when he comes -- he will continue only a short time.**

Beginning with verse ten, Scripture introduces two new important facts to this study. First, it warns that seven major powers will precede the eighth and last government called the beast kingdom. The second point is found in the opening comment: **"five are fallen, and one is, and the other** [the 7th government] **has not yet come."** This curious statement is a prophetic calendar numbering the kingdoms that must exist both before and after the destruction of Mystery Babylon. A warning found in the opening verse of this same study chapter: **"Come, I will show you the judgment of the great whore that sitteth upon many waters."**

Scripture is telling the Church in verse ten that five of these eight special governments will have fallen or lost their status as world powers when this city is destroyed. According to this text, Mystery Babylon will be destroyed between the fifth and sixth kingdoms on this mysterious list of nations. The sixth government will then lose its hold in the world to a seventh, the latter to rule for only a brief period prior to the eighth (and final) kingdom called the beast.

This critical list of eight kingdoms is examined in the following chapter, as Scripture now highlights the kingdom in power when Christ returns:

Vs. 11
And the beast that was, and is not, even he is the eighth -- and is of the seven -- and goeth into perdition.

Not only do the Scriptures imply for the third time in verse 11 that ancient Rome is not the source of this end-time beast government, but it also makes a critical comment about the beast in this text that is not mentioned in the previous verses. The eighth or last government on this mysterious list of kingdoms **"is of the seven."** In other words, it is comprised of all the previous seven kingdoms.

Seemingly there is only one way for this coalition to occur, and that is for the eighth government to be some kind of world order, one that would include all the previously mentioned kingdoms. Here again, the United Nations fulfills this important prophecy, as it has enrolled all of the nations of the world, including the territories of the seven kingdoms mentioned in verse 11.

Beginning in verse 12, Scripture again focuses on the ten horn kingdoms and their involvement with the beast government:

The Ten Horns

Vs. 12
And the ten horns which you saw are ten kings, who have no kingdom as yet, but receive power as kings one hour with the beast.

Vs. 13
These have one mind, and shall give their power and strength unto the beast.

As these verses add additional details about the "ten horns", they begin by implying that these ten men have immense political authority; however, it adds that their power will be limited to the time span of "**one hour**", a statement that implies that their association with the beast government is for a brief period.

As previously mentioned, New York City is hosting or "sitting" on a large world government called the United Nations. And within this body of nations is a much smaller group called the "Security Council". According to the UN Charter, this small but powerful 15-member committee not only has the obligation of being the peacekeeper to the world, but it also has substantial control over the entire UN General Assembly.

Within the structure of the 15-member Security Council is a third group of ten members who are temporary, or short term, representatives. These delegates are selected from within the UN General Assembly and are not to exceed two years of service as members on the Security Council. Their temporary appointment supports verse twelve's comment that these ten men are kings (or ambassadors), **"who have no kingdom** [or power on the Security Council] **yet, but receive power for one hour** [or short period] **with the beast."**

Currently the Security Council is made up of only five permanent members: The nations of Great Britain, France, China, Russia and the United States, two important members short of the needed number mentioned in verse seven as belonging to the beast government. Beginning in 1979, however, the UN General Assembly presented to the Security Council the question of equitable representation for its members and again increasing its membership. The structure of the Security Council has, in fact, changed several times in the past. The most recent was in August 1965 with the amendment of Article 23 which increased the temporary members from six to the present ten members.

As for the latest motion from the General Assembly to increase its membership, the UN Security Council thus far has not been very swift in acting on this recent proposal. In 1982, however, to show that they were open to this suggestion, the council did add Spanish and Arabic to its list of official languages. But due to the delicate political situation of the previous cold war, no new nations were officially added at that time. As a result, Rule

41 of the Security Council Rules of Procedure now reads: "Arabic, Chinese, English, French, Russian and Spanish shall be the official and working languages of the Security Council." It may be more than just a coincidence, as diagramed in the following chart, there are now two languages that do not represent nations with permanent status on the Security Council; Spanish and Arabic.

— THE UN SECURITY COUNCIL —
Permanent Members / Official Languages
& Year of Membership

1. G.B. = English	1942	5. France = French	1944
2. U.S.A. = English	1942	6. _____ = Arabic	1980
3. Russia = Russian	1942	7. _____ = Spanish	1980
4. China = Chinese	1942		

— TEN SHORT TERM MEMBERS —
Replaced every two years from
within UN General Assembly

1._____	1944	6. _____	1944
2._____	1944	7. _____	1965
3._____	1944	8. _____	1965
4._____	1944	9. _____	1965
5._____	1944	10. _____	1965

The only missing element at this time for the UN Security Council to fulfill Scripture, is two more permanent members on the Security Council. Considering the two new official working languages of this body, these would very probably be a Spanish and an Arabic speaking nation. With these two additions, as diagramed in the previous chart, this unique and powerful group of men will have fulfilled Bible prophecy. And in doing so provided the world with a government having "seven heads" and "ten [short term] horns."

When the chart of the Security Council is compared to Scriptures description of the Beast government, it reveals a probability that is both frightening and exhilarating. The Security Council's framework accurately mirrors all the Scriptural requirements to be the world's last government prior to Christ's return.

It should be noted here that due to the previously mentioned position of the United Nations of deliberately not giving recognition to God as its source of wisdom and strength to govern the world, the UN stands a good chance of fulfilling prophecy as Scripture now warns that in the last days, the beast government adopts an anti-Church policy:

Vs. 14
> These shall make war with the lamb, and the lamb shall overcome them; for he is the Lord of lords, and the King of kings, and they that are with him are called, the chosen, and the faithful.

Vs. 15

> And he said unto me, the waters that you saw where the harlot sits, are peoples, and multitudes, and nations, and tongues.

Vs. 16

> And the ten horns that you saw upon the beast, shall hate the harlot, and shall make her desolate and naked, and shall eat her flesh, and burn her with fire.

Vs. 17

> For God has put it in their hearts to fulfill his will, and to agree, and give their kingdom unto the beast. Until the words of God be fulfilled.

With verse fourteen's reference to **"these"**, and the statement **"that the lamb shall overcome them,"** Scripture again verifies that the beast is a government by committee with more than one member.

These verses also confirm the opening comments in this chapter about the **"harlot"** sitting on a very large population as it describes them as **"peoples, multitudes, nations and tongues,"** one that includes several nations and diverse languages. It should be noted that this description of Mystery Babylon not only fits New York City and its 83 different languages and dialects, but also applies to the 170-plus member nations of the UN General Assembly and the Security Council within it.

The angel also implies in these verses that all of the ten nations serving as horns in the beast government at the time of Mystery Babylon's death somehow have a role in this city's destruction. The question is: Are all ten horn members involved? Or is it that they only support this retaliatory action against the United States over some previous political decision, such as trade controls due to the U.S. deficit or the delicate Middle East problem which may have offended someone? The reason for this question is that Scripture later reveals that the antichrist may be the sole person responsible for this catastrophic accomplishment.

Scripture informs the Church in verse 17, however, that the allegiance of the ten horn nations to the beast government is essential, and that God permits this city to be destroyed. It is an encounter that ushers in unmanageable world problems and opens the door for the UN Security Council to exercise its authority as spelled out in the UN Charter.

As chapter 18 closes, it now identifies the harlot it was describing throughout this chapter, revealing that it is in reality a great city with unique control over the rulers of the earth:

Vs. 18
And the woman that you saw is that great city that reigns over the kings of the earth.

Scripture leaves little doubt should one still question the meaning of the term harlot as verse 18 clearly defines it as a great city with worldwide powers. It also states that this city will have some kind of control, or power over the "**kings** [or rulers] **of the earth.**" It should be noted that in the original text the word "reigns" can be interpreted to take care of someone, such as a nurse over a patient, or a host at some hotel or party. A comment that adds to the probability that New York City may in fact be, Mystery Babylon.

Summary: Revelation Chapter 17

Should John's description of Mystery Babylon be New York City, its promised destruction would do much more then destroy the lives of countless numbers of people. This world class city represents the financial heartbeat of the United States and most of the world as well, including banking, trust funds, the stock markets, and a host of other financial activities. And as outlined in Revelation 18, its ruin would cripple economically not only the United States, but the entire world.

A disaster to a financial center such as New York City would also create a serious problem to the world's balance of power, resulting in government structures throughout the world to fall. Thus the United Nations Security Council is brought closer to fully exercising its awesome power in retaining order and stabilizing a shattered world economy.

Time does not allow a detailed account of the many obligations outlined of the Security Council as defined in the UN Charter. It is essential, however, to consider a few examples to illustrate the magnitude of the council's power and influence within the world's political community.

Most people are not aware that the structure of the United Nations Charter requires that all members of the UN General Assembly give to the Security Council their full support. Article 25 states that "All members of the United Nations agree to accept and carry out the decisions of the Security Council according to the present Charter."

Further proof of their power and influence is found in Article 42. It confirms that as the world's peacekeeper, the Security Council is given the responsibility of evaluating any threat to world peace and shall judge what measures shall be taken, including any military action necessary against that nation they consider a threat. Article 43 of the UN Charter then adds to their immense power by stating that member nations of the UN and their military forces are to be at the disposal of the Security Council.

Article 97 is another example of authority given to the Security Council. It states that they are required to give their approval before any Secretary General is appointed as head of the United Nations by the General Assembly.

The question of the Security Council's power is not something that has just occurred. As early as 1944, this problem was brought up for discussion among the 50 members of this newly formed group called the "United Nations". In Dumbarton Oaks, outside Washington, D.C., UN members addressed this serious problem in a series of meetings in the fall of that year. They warned the then existing five members of the Security Council that it had, in fact, created another "Munich". This statement referred to a controversial meeting in Germany only a few years earlier (1938) between Chamberlain of Great Britain, Italy's fascist leader Mussolini, and Daladier representing France along with its host Adolf Hitler. Excluded from this gathering, however, was Czechoslovakia's President Benes, who, unable to fight for his country's legal right to the Sudentenland (her northern most territory), was forced to go along with the other western leaders allowing Germany the right to take over this portion of Czechoslovakia as Hitler's fee for peace in Europe. This ill-fated agreement in not limiting Hitler and calling his bluff, ultimately became the cause of World War II.

Because of this and other valid criticisms, the final outcome of the UN meetings in 1944 changed the format of the Security Council on several issues, beginning with six additional members added that same year to the five previous permanent member nations. These additional nations were temporary positions due to their being limited to serving only a single two-year term on the council, members who were selected from a rotating schedule within the entire UN General Assembly.

The United Nations was recognizing for the first time the inherent dangers within the Security Council due to the awesome power and authority it held, and it was now taking some safeguards against it, the most crucial being the office of the Security Council's President. This appointment would now rotate alphabetically between both its permanent and temporary members -- not to exceed one month per term.

As this study chapter concludes, there still remains the puzzling comment in Revelation 17:10-11 that the beast government will be the eighth world power on its list of special kingdoms. The question then arises: Is there support for this mysterious list of eight kingdoms elsewhere in Scripture and can it offer further information to the Church regarding the coming judgment to Mystery Babylon, or that of the antichrist?

This inquiry can be better answered in the following pages as this study directs its attention to the Old Testament.

Chapter IV

Israel's Inner and Outer Court

Shadows of his Coming

As the following pages prepare to explore the seventh chapter of Daniel and his comments about the four governments of flesh and the antichrist, it will be to the reader's advantage to first examine Daniel's second chapter outlining his four kingdoms of minerals.

The need for this companion study will prove vital when Revelation is again reviewed, for up to this time, most Bible scholars believed the kingdoms of flesh as nothing more than a repeat of his kingdoms of minerals, a theory this study will prove is seriously flawed.

This statement is made in light of the previous study of Revelation 17:11, where it stated that the beast government is the eighth kingdom, marking the return of Christ. A statement that comes into question when Daniel's seventh chapter is later examined as he identifies the beast government as being only the fourth kingdom. The probable solution to this contradiction is that Daniel's seventh chapter and the four kingdoms of flesh is not a supplement to his second chapter of minerals, but a totally different prophecy.

This theory is supported in the following verses as they prove crucial in unraveling Daniel's two visions. They also give a prophetic profile of the Holy Land between the two known periods of Israel's history.

Beginning with a brief look at Revelation's tenth chapter, verse 11 opens the door to this controversial subject. In this prophetic account, John is told to record for the Church signs and happenings that will concern both Christ's return and the future of Israel:

Revelation: Chapter 10
Vs. 11

> **And he** [the angel] **said unto me, thou must prophesy again before many peoples, and nations, and tongues, and kings.**

Revelation: Chapter 11
Vs. 1

> **And there was given unto me a reed like a rod: and the angel stood, saying, rise, and measure the temple of God, and the altar, and them that worship therein** [the inner court].

Vs. 2

> **But the court which is without the temple -- leave out, and measure it not; for it is given unto the gentiles: and the holy city shall they tread under foot forty and two months.**

78

Revelation records here that John was shown the Jewish Temple complete with both its inner and outer courts. And after being given a rod, John is told to measure only the inner court, that portion that contained the altar and those Jewish people honoring God within it. The outer court, or visitor's area of the Temple was ordered left unmeasured, or unrecorded.

Although not readily apparent, the command to measure only the Temple's inner court proves crucial to this study chapter. In this statement, Scripture offers to the Church the needed foundation for identifying Revelation's eight special kingdoms. These are governments that when later examined, not only parallel Daniel's two different accounts of minerals and flesh, but both Revelation and Daniel will then conclude with the beast government as the eighth and final kingdom in power before Christ returns.

Of equal importance is the need to examine the angel's charge concerning the "outer court", a mandate stating that this part of the Temple was to remain unmeasured. It is this mysterious directive to John and its correlation with the Holy Land that becomes the focus of the following pages.

Seven Thunders of The Outer Court

In Revelation 10:1-4, John also writes that he was allowed to witness seven future events, significant happenings he believed should be recorded and was about to do so until the angel stops him:

79

Revelation: Chapter 10
Vs. 1

And I saw another mighty angel come down from heaven, clothed with a cloud; and a rainbow was upon his head, and his face was as though it were the sun, and his feet like pillars of fire.

Vs. 2

And he had in his hand a little open book; and he set his right foot upon the sea, and his left foot upon the earth.

Vs. 3

And cried with a loud voice, as when a lion roareth; and when he had cried -- seven thunders uttered their voices,

Vs. 4

And when the seven thunders had uttered their voices, I was about to write; and I heard a voice from heaven saying unto me seal up those things which the seven thunders uttered.

In this text, a special messenger reveals seven incidents that caught John's interest, events he believed were important enough to include as part of this Scripture. But as he was about to describe them, a voice from heaven interrupts this scene, and is heard giving John instructions to identify them only as **"seven thunders."**

Interestingly, when examining the history of the Holy Land, evidence clearly points to seven stormy periods as a non-Jewish nation. These were the seven foreign armies of occupation that plagued Israel from the Temple's destruction in 70 A.D. through to the British evacuation in 1948.

It is this segment of Israel's history that is now examined in light of Revelation's reference to the "outer court."

The Thunders Begin

With the Romans destroying the Temple in 70 A.D. and many of Israel's leaders dead or exiled, the synagogue, an institution introduced by the returning Babylonian exiles six centuries earlier, again became the place of worship for the Jewish people. Then, in 130 A.D. the Roman Emperor Hadrian, upon visiting Jerusalem, discovered some very strong Jewish nationalistic feeling. Determined to crush it, he issued a series of anti-Jewish edicts. Among these orders was the banning of the Sabbath and the rite of Jewish circumcision, a move which ignited a nearly successful Jewish uprising against Rome between 132 and 135 A.D.

The outcome of this insurrection by the Jewish community culminated the first blow in this series of "thunders" to their beloved land, for it was at this time that Hadrian eradicated all Jewish culture from the city of Jerusalem, even giving it a new Roman name: "Aelia Capitolina". No Jewish person was to enter this new city, or come within view of it under the penalty of death.

The second storm to come to the Holy Land was in 324 A.D. When conquered by Constantine the Great, he made Jerusalem a Christian city and again named it Jerusalem. It remained such until 638 A.D. while during this time, the Jewish people were barred from it.

In 638 A.D. the Moslems took over the Holy Land under the caliph Omar, making it possible for the first time in over 500 years for Jewish people to enter their beloved city. However, when the Jewish community did not embrace the Moslem faith, many experienced persecution and hardship. This third period lasted until 1099.

A fourth era began when the crusaders took Israel and its treasured city from the Moslems (1099-1187). This new invader of the City of David proved to be less tolerant of the Jewish community than were the Moslems before them. In a bloody battle in 1099, they not only killed all the Moslems, but the Jewish people within the city as well, and again, the crusaders prevented the Jewish people from entering Jerusalem. This ban, however, was later lifted in the middle of the twelfth century.

Israel's fifth invaders were again the Moslems (1187-1517), beginning with Saladin, an Armenian Kurd. Following this famous leader were the Mamelukes -- a people made up of Mongols and Kurds as well as Turks and Circassians from Russia. Resuming possession of the Temple Mount, they rebuilt the city and its walls. With Jerusalem under control of this Moslem government, the Jewish people were given access to their beloved city. And again, they were subject to many restrictions, but those more tolerable then under the crusaders.

As the sixth invader, the Ottoman Empire controlled the Holy Land and the Temple Mount from 1517-1917. At its inception the Jewish people fared well, but as time went on, life for them grew harder. They suffered little of the persecution of their counterparts in the rest of the world, yet they were barred from the temple site. Unfortunately, in the latter years of the Ottoman Empire, the Jewish people were subjected to considerable bribery and extortion.

"The British Mandate, 1917-1948." Here begins the seventh and final occupation of Israel. In its beginning, little conflict appeared between Jew and Arab over this troubled land; However, with Israel's capture by the British in 1917, the world stage was set for a dynamic revival of this ancient land. Jewish hopes, nonetheless, were dampened when Arab hostility to a Jewish national home became evident. It also became obvious to both groups that one day they would come face-to-face over the issue of which of them would control this land.

With British control ending in 1948, history has witnessed seven foreign armies occupy both Israel and its capital prior to it becoming a nation again. It is this study's contention that these seven armies of occupations are the same "seven thunders" that John witnessed in Revelation 10:3, but was not permitted to identify or record by name or symbol. Governments that would bridge the gap between the first and second nations of Israel referred to in Revelation 11:2 as the "outer court". And, according to this text, kingdoms during this dark period of Israel's absence as a nation would not be recorded in Scripture.

Israel's Completed Inner And Outer Courts

Inner Court

Part II

The Four Kingdoms of
"**FLESH**"

1948 - Armageddon

The
"**SevenThunders**"
of the outer court
70 A.D. to 1948

No. 1 **Romans/Hadren**
70 A.D. - 324

No. 2 **Constantine**
324 - 638

No. 3 **Moslems**
638-1099

No. 4 **Crusaders**
1099 - 1187

No. 5 **Moslems**
1187 - 1517

No. 6 **Ottoman Empire**
1517 - 1917

No. 7 **Great Britain**
1917 - 1948

Inner Court

Part I

The Four Kingdoms of
"**MINERALS**"

550 B.C. - 70 A.D.

The accompanying chart illustrates how these seven intruders integrate into Israel's dark past and thus become a vital part of Jewish history.

Israel's Past and Present

Listed along with the outer court's seven thunders are two added columns arranged under the headings of Israel's "Inner Court", parts I and II. The first represents Israel beginning with Daniel's record 800 years before Christ through to 70 A.D. The second heading marked "Inner Court, Part II", represents the Holy Land from 1948 to the present.

To anyone who has studied prophecy, this chart will be unfamiliar, and some may question if Scripture has divided Israel's history into the proposed three columns. There is, however, Scripture to support this theory.

In Daniel's twelfth chapter beginning with verse four, Daniel records a summary of his vision of the last days and of the coming tribulation to the nation of Israel. According to this text, Daniel is standing along side the Tigris River when a messenger from heaven informs him that his ministry as a prophet is about to come to an end.

According to verse four, Daniel is ordered to close and seal his book with all of its warnings and prophecies, when in verse five, a new scene unfolds as two additional angels appear. While the first angel stood with Daniel on his side of the riverbank, the second angel, <u>standing on the other side of the river</u>, begins a discussion with the messenger about the last days and the future suffering of Israel as Daniel and the first angel were only allowed to listen:

Daniel: Chapter 12
Vs. 4

But thou, O Daniel, shut up the words, and seal the book, to the time of the end; many shall run to and fro, and knowledge shall be increased.

Vs. 5

Then I, Daniel, looked, and, behold, there stood two others, one on this side of the bank of the river, and the other on that side of the bank of the river.

Vs. 6

And [the one on the far side] said to the man clothed in linen, which was upon the waters of the river, how long shall it be to the end of these wonders?

Vs. 7

And I heard the man clothed in linen, which was on the waters of the river, when he held up his right hand and his left hand unto heaven, and swore by him who liveth forever, that it shall be for a time, times, and an half; [3-1/2 years] and when he shall accomplish the breaking up of the power of the holy people, all these things [the previous prophecies] shall be finished.

The messenger's comment here about the three and a half years of hardship for Israel is a direct reference to the days just prior to Christ's return and the invasion of Israel by the antichrist. It will be an assault that will focus on his attempt to destroy Israel as a nation.

Daniel, overcome with curiosity then asks the messenger in the following verse, what all of this would mean. But instead of an answer, Scripture implies that this incident does not concern him:

Vs. 8
And I heard, but I understood not. Then said I, my Lord, what shall be the end of these things?

Vs. 9
And he said, go thy way, Daniel; for the words are closed up and sealed until the time of the end.

Although was never allowed to know the meaning behind his vision of the two angels, the river that separated them, or the comment about the three and a half years of tribulation for the Jewish people, Scripture implies that there is a valuable message **"sealed"** in this prophetic account. A disclosure verse nine goes on to imply will be revealed to the Church in the last days.

Also crucial to this study is the fact that Daniel, upon inquiring about the events discussed on the other side of the river, was told to, **"Go thy way, for the words and their meaning are sealed until the time of the end."** As a result of this reply, it is conceivable that both Daniel and the angel standing with him symbolize the first kingdom of Israel. The river would then represent the outer court, that critical period between 70 A.D. and the 14th of May, 1948, when Israel would not be a Jewish state. The angel on the other side of the river, however, would represent Israel's second tenure as a sovereign nation, a period that began in 1948 and continues into the three and a half years of tribulation mentioned by the messenger in verse seven.

Nonetheless, the strongest evidence in support of Israel's two-part history record is yet to be found in the vast contrast between Daniel's second and seventh chapters. It is in these two records where the answer to unlocking the identity of the eight mystery kingdoms in Revelation 17 is established.

In the book of Daniel two series or sets of kingdoms are recorded, and contrary to past theories or interpretations, they are not duplications of the same four governments. They are instead a continuous record of eight individual kingdoms, governments that when fully explored, will exist only during Israel's two tenures as a sovereign nation.

This two-part record begins in chapter two with Daniel recording the four "mineral" governments of Israel's first period as a nation. They included the empires of gold, silver, bronze, and a fourth, described as iron mixed with clay. These four kingdoms coincide with Israel as a nation from the Babylonian Empire 800 years before Christ through to Israel's collapse in 70 A.D.

Corresponding to Israel becoming a nation in 1948, a second set of four kingdoms described as "flesh" are found in Daniel 7:1-28. Four world powers beginning with an alliance involving two governments, one being a Lion and the other an Eagle. These two nations are then succeeded by a Bear, followed by the Leopard, and last, Daniel's introduction of the Beast.

The kingdoms of flesh are examined in the next portion of this study, as the following pages focus on Daniel's second chapter and his four kingdoms of minerals beginning with verse 31.

The Kingdoms of Minerals

In Daniel's second chapter, Scripture records that King Nebuchadnezzar has had a disturbing dream. Due to the fact he could remember neither its details nor its meaning, the king presented the matter to his seers who also were unable to help, even under the threat of death. Daniel being told about the problem, then offers to help the king solve it. And after Daniel and his friends took the matter to the Lord in prayer, Daniel is given the dream along with its interpretation as he now shares it with the king:

Vs. 31
Thou, O king, sawest, and behold a great image. This great image, whose brightness was excellent, stood before thee; and the form thereof was terrible.

Vs. 32

This image's head was of fine gold, his breast and his arms of silver, his belly and his thighs of brass,

Vs. 33

His legs of iron, his feet part of iron, part of clay.

Vs. 34

Thou sawest till that a stone was cut without hands, which smote the image upon his feet that were of iron and clay, and brake them to pieces.

Vs. 35

Then was the iron, the clay, the brass, the silver, the gold, broken to pieces together, and became like the chaff of the summer threshing floors; and the wind carried them away, that no place was found for them; and the stone that smote the image became a great mountain, and filled the whole earth.

In this account, Daniel reveals to the king all the details of his distressing dream, an interpretation that begins with the dream's head of gold down to its feet of iron and clay. The king is also told about a stone which Scripture implies is just average in size, a stone cut without (human) hands that will one day strike this series of kingdoms on its feet of iron and clay.

The drama that Daniel interprets for the King is a prophecy, with the stone in verse 34 representing the birth of the Church. Daniel then adds that after the Church enters the scene, the four mineral kingdoms collapse. Their remains become as dust, never to rise again. Of interest here is that following the collapse of the four minerals, the stone grows in size to where Scripture describes it as a **"great mountain"**, one that in its future **"filled the whole earth."** It is a prophecy that mirrors the early Church as it began its journey into a worldwide kingdom of believers.

Daniel then interprets the mysterious dream for the king beginning with verse 36:

Vs. 36
This is the dream, and we will tell its interpretation before the king.

Vs. 37
Thou, o king, art a king of kings; for the God of heaven hath given thee a kingdom, power, and strength, and glory.

Vs. 38
And wherever the children of men dwell, the beast of the field and the fowls of the heavens hath he given into thine hand, and hath made thee ruler over them all -- thou art this head of gold.

Vs. 39
And after thee shall arise another kingdom inferior to thee [silver], and another third kingdom of bronze, which shall bear rule over all the earth.

Daniel not only assures the king (and the Church) that the Babylonian government is the first kingdom on the list described as the head of gold, but Daniel also reveals the two additional kingdoms that must one day follow his Babylonian Empire: The kingdoms of silver and bronze.

History records the kingdom of silver was the Mede and Persian alliance that later overran the Babylonians. And like the first example, the kingdom of silver was an important world empire during Israel's first tenure as a nation.

Daniel described the third kingdom as bronze. This proved to be the ancient Kingdom of Greece which followed the Medo-Persian Empire. And again, as a world power, it also existed along with the nation of Israel.

Beginning with the following verse, Daniel, introduces a fourth government. It is a kingdom that not only has the strength of iron, but is tainted with clay:

Vs. 40

And the fourth kingdom shall be strong as iron, for as much as iron breaketh in pieces and subdueth all things; and, as iron that breaketh all these, shall it break in pieces and bruise.

Vs. 41

And whereas thou sawest the feet and toes, part of potters clay and part of iron, the kingdom shall be divided; but there shall be in it of the strength of the iron, for as thou sawest the iron mixed with clay.

Vs. 42

And as the toes of the feet were part of iron and part of clay, so shall the kingdom be partly strong and partly broken.

Vs. 43

And whereas thou sawest iron mixed with miry clay, they [the kings of iron] shall mingle themselves with the seed of [common] men; but they shall not adhere to another, even as iron is not mixed with clay.

Verse 40 begins this segment noting that the Kings representing the two feet and ten toes of the fourth kingdom are made of two minerals. It begins with iron which represents their power and strength, and in verse 41, clay is added, a substance which according to this passage, dangerously weakens their kingdom.

Unfortunately, because Daniel's upcoming seventh chapter of flesh has been assumed to be a supplement to this account in chapter two, little attention has been given to the two feet that Scripture includes along with the ten toes in verse 41. As a result, important historic details have been overlooked, facts that when examined, support this study's contention that Daniel's second chapter describing the four mineral kingdoms has nothing to do with the four flesh kingdoms of chapter seven, or with Christ's return.

If then, one is willing to set aside temporarily Daniel's seventh chapter and its description of four governments of flesh, the question arises: What would one look for within the infrastructure of the Roman Empire at the time of the Christ that could possibly explain Scripture's mention of the clay being added to the iron -- or its mention of the two feet?

Kings of Iron and Clay

History records that just before and during the time of Christ and His apostles, Rome had been governed by a series of 12 emperors. Six of which were a powerful and unique family called the Julio-Claudians. It was a dynasty that began with Julius Caesar in 44 B.C. and ended with Nero in 68 A.D. What makes this subject worth noting is that following Nero's death, the next six emperors were selected from ordinary people within the Roman Senate, thus fulfilling verse 43.

To better explain their connection to this study, a list is shown on p.95 containing the names of these 12 Roman Emperors and the period of their reign beginning with Julius Caesar in 44 B.C. and ending with Domitian in 96 A.D.

Making this list meaningful is that it exposes how these 12 rulers (two feet and ten toes) are divided into kings of iron and kings of clay.

Adding to this disclosure, is that when the emperors are closely examined, the twelfth person was Domitian. And it was during Domitian's reign as emperor that John, the author of Revelation and the last of the 12 original Apostles of Christ, is presumed to have died.

The Two Feet And Ten Toes Of Daniel 2:41.

"The Kings Of Iron"
(Julio-Claudians)

1.	Julius Caesar	44 B.C. - 42 B.C.
2.	Augustus	27 B.C. - 14 A.D.
3.	Tiberius	A.D. 14 - 37
4.	Caligula	37 - 41
5.	Claudius	41 - 54
6.	Nero	54 - 68

"The Kings Of Clay"
(Commoners)

7.	Galba	68 - 69
8.	Otho	69 (4 mo.)
9.	Vitellius	69 (8 mo.)
10.	Vespasian	69 - 79 *
11.	Titus	79 - 81 *
12.	Domitian	81 - 96

Aside from Domitian witnessing the death of the last apostle, the chart exposes the emperors responsible for breaking up the nation of Israel and destroying Jerusalem and its temple. Vaspasion*, a military commander at the time, initiated the battle against the rebellious Jewish people in 68 A.D., but due to his being called back to Rome to become their tenth emperor, Titus* was then appointed to complete the task in 69 A.D.

This period of Israel's history was also marked by these two men's ruthless capture of the moun-

tain fortress called "Mesada". A mountain strong-
hold containing a large settlement of Jewish rebels
that has now become a symbol for the Jewish
people and their will to survive in their new nation.

Looking back into Israel's past, it is very likely
that Vaspasion and Titus are symbolized by the two
feet mentioned in Daniel 2:41-42. The two men who
were responsible for stomping out Israel's flame of
national identity.

Assuming that John's death did actually take
place during Domitians reign as Rome's twelfth
emperor, the list of 12 emperors would then fulfill
Daniel's prophecy in verse 44 regarding the birth of
the Church:

The Birth of The Church

Vs. 44

> **And in the days of these kings** [the two feet
> and ten toes] **shall the God of heaven set up
> a kingdom, which shall never be destroyed;
> and the kingdom shall not be left to other
> people, but it shall brake in pieces and
> consume all these kingdoms, and it shall
> stand forever.**

Besides the assertion that there are 12 kings, is
the attached phrase in verse 44 that a kingdom is
"set up" at this time. In this text the idiom "set
up" translates as: "to appoint someone in a new
business or some long-term building project." This
factor was verified in verse 35 where it said that

the stone that caused the great image to fall, "**then** [or later] **became a great mountain.**" It is a prophecy that refers to Christ as the rock, who with his followers would in time grow to become a mountain that would fill the whole earth.

Expanding on this verse is the word "**kingdom**" when it is examined in the light of Christ's own teachings. Matthew 4:17 documents that from the earliest beginnings of His ministry, Christ proclaimed that "The kingdom of God is at hand."

Further clarifying this statement is Romans 14:17 there the Apostle Paul explains just what the "kingdom" of Christ represents: "For the kingdom of God is not food or drink, but [these unseen things] righteousness -- peace -- and the joy of the Holy Spirit."

Over the past centuries, Romans 14:17 has not only proven to be one of the foundation blocks of the gospel of Jesus Christ, but it has fulfilled Daniel's prophecy. The gospel has far surpassed all other previous religions. This includes ideologies that began with the Babylonians, further developed by the Medo-Persians and Greek Empires and employed by the Romans in setting the world's religious and moral standards before Christ. This fact may well explain why all four minerals were described as visible and standing when the Church was originally introduced as the rock in verse 34. And according to verse two of this chapter, the Church has since caused their religious philosophies to "**become like the chaff of the summer thrashing floors.**"

As chapter two concludes, Daniel not only confirms that Christ's birth will be unique, but he also adds that Christ's birth will greatly affect the world's religions from this time on as they no longer draw from the past beliefs and superstitions:

Vs. 45

For as much as thou sawest the stone was cut out of the mountain without hands, and that it broke in pieces the [spiritual darkness of] **iron, the bronze, the silver, and the gold, the great god has made known to the king what shall come to pass from now on; and the dream is certain, and the interpretation of it sure.**

Religious historians agree that there is little attraction left in any of the mentioned philosophies offered by the four mineral kingdoms. There is, however, overwhelming evidence that Church has become the **"mountain"** that Scripture prophesied it would be. This is supported in the following pages as overlooked facts relating to this chapter are examined.

Summary: Daniel, Chapter Two

In the study of Daniel's second chapter and his record of four mineral kingdoms, it was established that all four governments were major world powers in order of their sequence, and that all four kingdoms existed during Israel's first tenure as a nation.

Unfortunately, verses 41 through 44 in Daniel's second chapter have misled many regarding the government in power when Christ returns. Up to this time, it has been widely accepted that these verses referred to the Lord's second coming, confusing the ten toes of this text with the ten horns recorded in Revelation 17.

However, verse 41 included the two feet as also being essential to this government of iron and clay. This makes a total of not ten, but 12 rulers that the Church should be looking for. And in lieu of this statement, history has some interesting facts that should be explored at this time; a study that will offer additional insight about the prophecy concerning Rome's government of iron being contaminated with clay:

According to all accounts, the Roman Empire had been governed by a powerful and unique family between 44 B.C. and 68 A.D. A dynasty of six emperors previously identified as the Julio-Claudians.

FAMILY TREE OF THE JULIO-CLAUDIANS

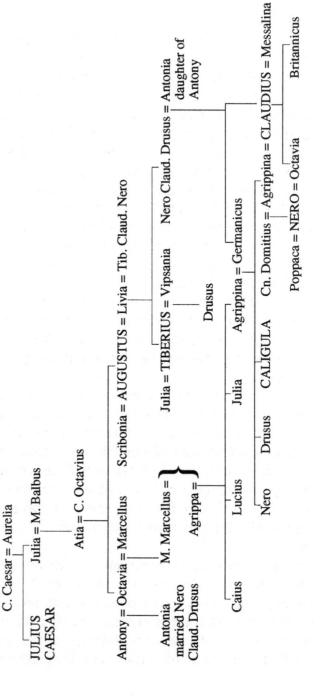

On the accompanying page is the Julio-Claudian family tree outlining their relationship to each other, and most notably, the intermarriages that took place among them. A fact that may have contributed greatly to Nero's mental state and bizarre abuse of power. Among these abuses was his having Britannicus, a future heir to the empire, murdered as a young child.

With Britannicus murdered and history recording that Nero died childless, no successor was left to carry on his family's control of the Roman Empire. As a result, emperors after Nero were chosen from within the Roman senate. It is important to note that like most of the previous Julio-Claudians, the next six emperors witnessed the founding of the early Church while the apostles were alive (note chart on p. 96). A shared existence that concluded with John on the Isle of Patmos during the reign of Domitian.

The time of John's death and it coming under Domitian's rule as emperor is critical to this study in that it fulfilled a very important prophecy: **"In the days of these kings** [the ten toes and two feet of iron and clay] **shall the God of heaven set up a kingdom."** A fulfilled prophecy that supports the theory that the ten toes have nothing to do with the ten horns examined in later chapters.

As for Scripture's command in Revelation 10:4 not to record **"the seven thunders"**, one may correctly assume it was because these seven invading nations represented the outer court, that portion of Israel's history "given to the gentiles" recorded in Revelation 11:42. The four kingdoms of

101

Israel's Completed Inner And Outer Courts

Inner Court
Part I
The Four Kingdoms of
"**Minerals**"
550 B.C. - 70 A.D.

No. 1 **GOLD**
Babylonians

No. 2 **SILVER**
Medo/Persians

No. 3 **BRONZE**
Greek Empire

No. 4 **IRON/CLAY**
Roman Empire

The
"**SevenThunders**"
of the outer court
70 A.D. to 1948

No. 1 **Romans/Hadren**
70 A.D. - 324

No. 2 **Constantine**
324 - 638

No. 3 **Moslems**
638-1099

No. 4 **Crusaders**
1099 - 1187

No. 5 **Moslems**
1187 - 1517

No. 6 **Ottoman Empire**
1517 - 1917

No. 7 **Great Britain**
1917 - 1948

Inner Court
Part II
The Four Kingdoms of
"**Flesh**"
1948 - Armageddon

minerals, however, were fully described in Daniel's second chapter, four governments that existed during Israel's first interim as a nation.

To help bring this portion of Daniel's second chapter into perspective with Israel's inner and outer court, the chart on p.102, places them in order of their existence under the heading of the "inner court", part I, as Revelation implies in chapter 11, verses 1-2.

Assuming that the chart outlining Israel's inner and outer court represents a valid theory, then there are still four governments unaccounted for, four kingdoms that would not only be documented within Scripture, but would also coexist with the new state of Israel beginning with the year 1948. With attention focusing on this critical period along with its many implications, Daniel's seventh chapter is now examined as he offers the critical details necessary to unlocking this two-part mystery.

Chapter V

The Completed
Inner Court

Shadows of his Coming

In the second chapter of Daniel, four kingdoms portrayed as minerals were examined. The first was described as gold and identified as the ancient Babylonians, followed by silver representing the Medo/Persians, bronze as Greece, and iron and clay as the Roman Empire. History verifies that all four governments existed while Israel was a nation before the first century.

As the focus of this study is directed to Daniel's seventh chapter and his description of the flesh kingdoms, it is confronted with the fact that previous generations regarded chapter seven as a duplication of Daniel's first vision of minerals. The kingdoms of flesh was believed to be a repeat of the four kingdoms of minerals of chapter two, but with strikingly different details.

Then in 1948, Israel again became a nation. And with this historic event, the Church was given ample cause to examine Daniel's seventh chapter from a totally new and different perspective. This is especially apparent in light of the previous study of the seven thunders (Revelation 10:4), and the angel's command to John in Revelation 11:1-2 to measure only the inner court of the Temple.

In addition to these two passages of Scripture, the previous study of Revelation 17:10-14 remains the most challenging evidence against combining Daniel's two chapters into one time frame. It was here that Scripture warned that eight distinctive governments would precede the return of Christ. And, when Daniel's seventh chapter is closely examined, details describing the governments of flesh are found in question when aligned with the previous vision of minerals. These differences become so obvious, that Daniel will later inquire about them in verse 15.

Among the differences is not only the fact that the kingdoms of minerals are replaced with governments described as flesh, but chapter seven implies that all or most of the governments in Daniel's vision of flesh kingdoms will be in power when Christ returns.

Also, unlike the four kingdoms of minerals given to King Nebuchadnezzar which needed an intercessor in order to be fully explained in chapter two, Daniel will be the only one to witness the second vision of flesh kingdoms in chapter seven.

Acknowledging the mineral kingdoms as valid governments up to 70 A.D. and Israel's collapse as a nation, the following pages will confirm that beginning with 1948, and Israel's rebirth, the kingdoms of flesh are the four missing governments required to fulfill Revelation 17:11.

Supporting this theory are the opening verses of chapter seven. Here Daniel not only records that a second set of four governments will be raised, but he indicates that at the time of their introduction, "heavenly" winds are blowing upon the sea of humanity in all directions. Should these winds from above represent the Holy Spirit as recorded in Acts 2:2, the angel could be implying that in the age of the flesh kingdoms, there will be worldwide interest in the gospel of Christ:

Four Kingdoms of Flesh

Vs. 1

In the first year of Belshazzar, King of Babylon Daniel had a dream and visions upon his bed; then he wrote the dream, and told the sum of the matters.

Vs. 2

Daniel spake and said, I saw in my vision by night, and, behold, the four winds of the heaven strove upon the great sea.

Vs. 3

And four great beasts came up from the sea, diverse one from another.

Vs. 4

The first was like a lion, and it had eagle's wings: I beheld till the wings thereof were plucked, and it was lifted up from the earth, and made stand

> upon the feet of a man, and a man's
> heart was given to it.

Beginning with these verses, Daniel introduces his second set of kingdoms. He identifies them as animals, four descriptions of flesh, that according to the laws of science, would have little chance of successfully intermixing with the kingdoms of minerals in chapter two.

The first kingdom in this new series is described as a world power that embraces two powerful nations, one represented by a lion and the other by an eagle. But as Daniel studies this alliance, he notes that the eagle's wings are torn from the lion, leaving the latter to carry on alone in the forefront of world politics as a human heart is given to it.

Vs. 5

> And behold another beast, a second, like to a bear, and it raised up itself on one side, and it had three ribs in the mouth of it between the teeth of it: and they said thus unto it, arise, devour much flesh.

Following the lion and eagle alliance, Daniel describes a bear as the second world power in this series. He also adds an interesting footnote, one that implies that immediately following the eagle's removal from power, the bear is assumed to be in a passive, or harmless posture. However, the bear's peaceful appearance changes in verse five as Daniel records "it raised itself up" into an upright position having three ribs in its mouth.

It is important to note here that there is a strong probability that the eagle retains some official presence after its downfall as a nation. The comment "they said unto it -- arise and devour much flesh," suggests that both the eagle and the lion encourage the bear in its aggression, either by word of encouragement or, more likely, by not being strong enough to stop it.

The reference in verse five about the bear raising itself up after the eagle's removal also suggests that as one of the world's leading powers, the bear is considered a peaceful nation before this incident. Nonetheless, it is clearly a nation to be feared. This probability rests in the fact that the most dreaded parts of the bear are its front claws, weapons which can be brutal and are referred to again in a later prophecy.

Vs. 6

> **After this I beheld, and lo another, like a leopard, which had upon the back of it four wings of a fowl; the beast had also four heads; and dominion was given unto it.**

The third kingdom in this series of flesh is described in verse six as a leopard. Although this government is not easily identified at this time, the four heads and four wings add up to a possible total of eight separate nations belonging to this alliance. This powerful coalition is further explored in the following pages.

A Government Unlike Any Other

In the following verse, Daniel concludes his second vision by describing a government unlike anything he has seen before:

Vs. 7

> **After this I saw in the night visions, and behold a fourth beast, dreadful and terrible, and strong exceedingly; and it had great iron teeth: it devoured and brake in pieces, and stamped the residue with the feet of it: and it was different from all the beasts that were before it; and it had ten horns.**

Aside from the fact that the last government will have ten (horn) nations that add to its power and authority, Daniel notes that it will be **"different from all of the previous kingdoms before it."** According to verse seven, it will be a government that not only has great power in its decrees (its iron teeth), but even more in its claws which represent its military might.

Looking briefly into the next study chapter, Scripture adds some crucial information about this last government. Revelation 13:2 states that this worldwide empire it also calls "the beast", is represented by all the governments in Daniel's seventh chapter, except for the eagle. This unique alliance will have the body of the leopard, the feet (and claws) from the bear, and the lion's mouth (or head). Then in support of this coalition, Revelation includes the previously mentioned ten horns of verse seven -- adding that each horn is wearing a crown from their represented governments.

It is these ten governments that Daniel now focuses on in verse eight as he introduces the antichrist who arises out of this organization:

The Coming Antichrist

Vs. 8

I considered the horns, and, behold, there came up among them another little horn, before whom there were three of the first horns plucked up by the roots: and, behold, in this horn were the eyes like the eyes of a man, and a mouth speaking great things.

Daniel not only implies here that the ten horns represent ten smaller kingdoms, but he further notes that the antichrist will arise out of this unique group of men. However, before the antichrist comes into power, a twofold condition is attached to this warning. First, Daniel implies that the ten horn members must be an official arm of the beast government. And, following their belonging to this organization, three of these ten men are violently removed from office by the antichrist.

Scripture adds, however, that the antichrist is then cast into hell while the remaining members of the beast government are pardoned:

111

Vs. 9

> I beheld till the thrones were cast down, and the ancient of days did sit, whose garment was white as snow, and the hair of his head like the pure wool: his throne like the fiery flame, and his wheels fire.

Vs. 10

> A fiery stream issued and came forth from before him: thousand thousands ministered unto him, and ten thousand times ten thousand stood before him: the judgment was set, and the books were opened.

Vs. 11

> I beheld then because the voice of the great words which the horn spoke: I beheld till the beast was slain, and his body destroyed, and given to the burning flame.

Vs. 12

> As concerning the rest of the beasts, they had their dominion taken away: yet their lives were prolonged for a season and a time.

Pictured in these verses is the throne of heaven as thousands minister before God. It is during this scene of adulation that Daniel adds in verse 11 that he became interested in the antichrist, so much in fact that he could not take his eyes off the antichrist until he is judged and cast into hell.

However, Daniel's account of the antichrist's last hours presents a challenge to those who believe that his kingdoms of flesh are in some fashion, a repeat of his vision of minerals, for Daniel implies here that all (or most) of these governments identified as flesh are politically active and in power when Christ returns to set up His earthly realm.

The statement in verse 12, **"As for the rest of the beasts,"** strongly suggests that delegates from the kingdoms of the lion, the bear, and the leopard, along with the remaining horns, will be alive when Christ returns. It further indicates that as world leaders sharing power with the antichrist, they lose only their authority and control in this coalition. Their lives are spared when the Church's rule begins.

This unexplained pardon is examined in the following pages as Daniel now gives special notice to the coming Messiah and His promised world government:

A Vision of Glory

Vs. 13

> **I saw in the night visions, and, behold, one like the Son of man came with the clouds of heaven, and came to the Ancient of days, and they brought him near before him.**

Vs. 14

> And there was given him dominion, and
> glory, and a kingdom, that all people,
> nations, and languages, should serve
> him: his dominion is an everlasting
> dominion, which shall not pass away,
> and his kingdom that which shall not
> be destroyed.

Beginning with verse 13 Daniel describes the
Christ and coming Messiah being presented before
His Father in heaven as our Lord now receives
authority to govern the world's kingdoms.

The following verses note, however, that after
Daniel witnesses this heavenly display, he is deeply
troubled about the other visions and their connection to this heavenly coronation:

Vs. 15

> I, Daniel, was grieved in my spirit in
> the midst of my body, and the visions of
> my head troubled me.

Vs. 16

> I came near unto one of them that
> stood by, and asked him the truth of all
> this. So he told me, and made me know
> the interpretation of the things.

Vs. 17

> These great beasts, which are four, are
> four kings, who shall arise out of the
> earth.

Vs. 18

> But the saints of the most high shall
> take the kingdom, and possess the king-
> dom forever, even forever and ever.

This text records that Daniel's visions "**trou-bled**" him extensively, so severely in fact that Scripture adds that he walked over to a nearby angel to inquire about it. Although this text does not record his question to the angel, it can be safely assumed from the angel's answer that Daniel's vision of flesh concerned him because he realized that it had little in common with his previous vision of minerals.

"**These great beasts which are four, shall arise out of earth** [in the future]." It is in this simple response to Daniel that his concern about the second vision was apparently put to rest, as there was no other comments from him about it.

The angel's answer is confirmed when it is read in conjunction with the opening comment of this seventh chapter; "**In the first year** [of the reign] **of Belshazzar, King of Babylon, Daniel had a dream.**" History verifies that within nine years after Daniel received this second vision, the Medes and Persian alliance successfully conquered the Babylonian kingdom, thus ending their thousand year reign by dethroning Belshazzar.

With this fact in mind, it is doubtful that the angel would have told Daniel in verse 17 that four kingdoms would one day arise when history reveals one of them was about to collapse. And considering the downfall of the Babylonian Kingdom following closely behind Daniel's second vision, the angel's reply that the kingdoms of flesh **"who shall arise"** implies they are not a repeat of the four governments of minerals, but are instead, an addition to them. Again, Revelation 17:11 supports this assertion in its comment that this same beast government described by Daniel in verse seven, is not the fourth, but the eighth on its list of kingdoms.

Despite the angel's answer to Daniel, he still has questions regarding the antichrist and the ten horns that will be under his control:

Teeth of Iron and Nails of Bronze

Vs. 19

> **Then I would know the truth of the fourth [flesh] beast, which was diverse from all the others, exceedingly dreadful, whose teeth were of iron, and nails of bronze which devoured, broke in pieces, and stamped the residue with its feet.**

Vs. 20

> **And of the ten horns that were in its head, and of the other which came up, and before whom three fell; even of that horn that had eyes, and a mouth that spoke very great things, whose look was more stout then its fellows.**

Although Scripture does not specifically give the full meaning of either the iron teeth or the claws of bronze, the first probably represents the power and authority this government will have in its laws and decrees. The bronze claws would then represent the elite military power it will have at its disposal when it cannot assume control by legislation alone, claws that the following study chapter reveals belong to the bear.

According to Daniel, three of the ten horns are removed at this time, either personally by the antichrist or by some indirect covert action. This bold and cunning move by the antichrist then opens the door for his coming into power. And according to this verse, once he is in office, he makes a name for himself by becoming more involved regarding the issues of his day than have any of the preceding (horn) representatives.

As previously mentioned, the ten horns are only a small part of the beast government's power base. They are critical, nonetheless, in that the antichrist uses this secondary office as a back door to his taking control of this worldwide bureaucracy. Should the UN Security Council be this governing body, the loss of three of its representatives would be in direct violation of its charter (Article 23) and its requirement to have ten temporary members on this committee at all times. However, this apparent offence is corrected in Revelation 13:11.

In this Revelation account of the beast government, John records a scene describing the antichrist as he becomes part of this world organization: "**And I beheld another beast** [the antichrist] **coming out of the earth; and he had** [with him] **two horns like a lamb.**" The two horns described as lambs (or political pawns), are two additional horn

117

members that come into office along with the antichrist. These two added diplomats, along with the antichrist, are essential to the infrastructure of the Security Council, for by their admittance on the council, the previous charter violation described in verse 20 is corrected.

As the verses in Daniel continue, Scripture warns the Church of the coming antichrist and of his great hate for her:

The Despised Church

Vs. 21

> I beheld and the same horn made war with the saints, and prevailed against them.

Vs. 22

> Until the Ancient of days came, and judgment was given to the saints of the most High; and the time came that the saints possessed the kingdom.

Vs. 23

> Thus he said, the fourth beast shall be the fourth kingdom upon the earth, which shall be diverse from all kingdoms, and shall devour the whole earth, and shall tread it down, and break it in pieces.

During the antichrist's administration of the beast government, Scripture warns of testing and hardship for the Church. To those who believe in an early rapture of the Church, these warnings of adversity may not sound too alarming. On the other hand, should Scripture be describing the Church prior to Christ's return, it would be wise to examine these verses very carefully.

Daniel clearly states that the Church will be in opposition to the antichrist and his worldwide dominion. And, according to verse 22, this period of conflict lasts **"until the ancient of days came,"** referring to Christ's return.

Verse 23 then returns to the subject of the beast government with a statement that can easily be misinterpreted. It notes again that the beast kingdom is the fourth government in this series of flesh kingdoms, which, when added to the four kingdoms of minerals, the beast kingdom becomes the eighth government as prescribed in Revelation.

It should also be noted that verse 23 adds that this last government conquers the world and breaks it into pieces, a statement that could easily apply to the UN and its 170 plus members. These are participants that also have an important role as **"horns"** within this government. And according to the following verse, they play a major part in allowing the antichrist to come into power:

Vs. 24

> **And the ten horns out of this kingdom are ten kings that shall arise; and another shall arise after them, and he**

shall be diverse from the first, and he shall subdue three kings.

Vs. 25

And he shall speak great words against the most High, and shall wear out the saints of the most High, and think to change the times and the laws; and they shall be given unto his hand until a time and times and the dividing of times [3 1/2 years].

Vs. 26

But the judgment shall sit; and they shall take away his dominion, to consume and to destroy unto the end.

Vs. 27

And the kingdom and dominion, and the greatness of the kingdom under the whole heaven, shall be given to the people of the saints of the most High, whose kingdom is an everlasting kingdom, and all dominions shall serve and obey him.

As Scripture begins its review of the beast government, it also includes the ten horn nations that will be represented within it. Of special note is the statement that the ten horns **"shall arise"**, confirming that they come into power only after this world government has been established. Daniel further states that they are then followed by the antichrist who, according to verse 20, suggests that he will somehow be responsible for the downfall of three of them. This accusation of his involvement in these three deaths is examined in the following pages as Daniel now concludes this chapter:

Vs. 28

> **Here is the end of the matter, as for me, Daniel, my cogitations much troubled me, and my countenance changed in me; but I kept the matter in my heart.**

With the phrase, **"Here is the end of the matter,"** Daniel concludes his report. And although it is wished that there could be more information to fully understand this chapter, enough is written here when examined with the book of Revelation, to clearly identify these four great governments and the period in which they will exist.

Summary: Daniel Chapter Seven

In several verses throughout the New Testament, Scripture instructs the Church to "watch for the signs" of our Lord's return. When examined, the word "watch" is actually a command denoting some kind of action, such as studying the Scriptures for its warnings. It also suggests that one should remain aware of world events in light of Scripture's signs and warnings.

There has been a change, however, in the Church's position regarding the command to watch. It has instead allowed itself to be content to just wait for Christ's return. From this position, waiting is found to be a much safer position, especially when one looks at the many failures of past generations regarding the false identity of the beast government or that of the antichrist.

Should one be bold enough, however, to take the time to examine the Scriptures in light of recent history, it would take very little effort to come to some eye-opening conclusions. As previously noted, verse one's comment stating that Daniel alone received the second vision. This fact could be an additional key to help in placing the two visions into their proper periods within Church chronology. In the Old Testament it was essential to have an intercessor before coming before our Father in heaven. And, in Daniel's first vision, his mineral kingdoms were also given with need of an intercessor (King Nebuchadnezzar).

It is well recognized that in the New Testament, this need no longer exists, for through Christ and His death at Calvary, the Church now has a direct route to the Father in heaven. And, due to this uninterrupted access, Daniel's second set of flesh kingdoms may also have been given directly -- without the need of an intercessor.

Support for keeping Daniel's two sets of kingdoms as separate accounts, can also be found in Numbers 21:8. In this Old Testament account of redemption for the Jewish nation, a representation of sin is found described as a bronze serpent raised up on a staff. A symbol constructed of minerals that preceded the flesh and blood of Christ raised up on the cross at Calvary.

Besides the different backgrounds of the two visions, Daniel described the "lion" as having wings from an "eagle". When comparing these two symbols as coats-of-arms from the twentieth century, modern history confirms that many agreements and joint ventures have occurred between the lion of the British Commonwealth and the United State's eagle.

Looking at Daniel's sixth government which was described as a "bear", one government will generally come to mind, the Russian nation. The fact that Daniel first described this government in a passive position may be only a coincidence in light of Russia's recent policy of democratic change within it. It is clear, however, that the bear's nonaggressive position is short-lived because following the eagle's downfall as a nation, the bear is described with three ribs in its mouth. These three ribs could easily represent three of the nations Russia previously relinquished in its bid to become a free democratic society, nations such as those in the Baltic or Black Sea areas which would again give it access to the open sea throughout the entire year.

Following the bear, Daniel describes a "**leopard**" as the seventh government in this series. Its four heads and four wings suggest that it is made up of eight nations. Although it is not fully identified at this time, the Middle East may be a good place to look for such a coalition, especially when one considers how the world has become increasingly dependent upon oil from this important area. As a result, the eight oil-exporting nations within the powerful Arab League could easily become Daniel's seventh world power as they have in their control over half the world's oil and gas reserves.

Last is Daniel's eighth government. Scripture states that it will be totally different from all the previous kingdoms. According to verse 23, this unique government will be global in structure, breaking the world up into multiple members.

Presently, there is only one government that can fulfill this prophecy. That government is the United Nations because it has successfully enlisted almost every nation on earth, including the previous seven kingdoms prescribed in Revelation 17:11.

One should also keep in mind that the United Nations General Assembly is not controlled by its own participants as much as it is indirectly governed by the Security Council within it. It is this small but powerful group of permanent members and their ten affiliates who in reality, control much of the UN and its decisions regarding international affairs.

In defense of the UN's role in prophecy, p.126 contains an updated chart of Israel's inner and outer courts. When the two columns of the inner court are examined, the chart supports the theory that Daniel's two visions are Israel's completed "Inner Court" of Revelation 11:1. This fact becomes noticeably evident in that the chart also designates Daniel's beast kingdom as the world's eighth and last government in accord with Revelation 17:10-11:

Vs. 10
> **And** [or before which,] **there are seven kings** [kingdoms], **five are fallen, and one is, and the other has not yet come** --

Vs.11
> **And the beast that was, and is not, even he** [or it] **is the eighth, and is of the seven** [previous kingdoms].

In addition to Daniel's prophecy being better defined, the completed chart brings into the forefront John's comment in Revelation 17:10 about the fifth and sixth kingdoms. A comment that supports his opening statement of that same chapter:

Israel's Completed Inner And Outer Courts

Inner Court

Part I
The Four Kingdoms of "MINERALS"
550 B.C. - 70 A.D.

No.1 **GOLD** Babylonians

No. 2 **SILVER** Medo/Persians

No. 3 **BRONZE** Greek Empire

No. 4 **IRON/CLAY** Roman Empire

The "SevenThunders" of the outer court 70 A.D. to 1948

No.1 **Romans/Hadren** 70 A.D. - 324

No. 2 **Constantine** 324 - 638

No. 3 **Moslems** 638-1099

No. 4 **Crusaders** 1099 - 1187

No. 5 **Moslems** 1187 - 1517

No. 6 **Ottoman Empire** 1517 - 1917

No. 7 **Great Britain** 1917 - 1948

Inner Court

Part II
The Four Kingdoms of "FLESH"
1948 - Armageddon

No.5 **LION/EAGLE** G.B./U.S.A.

No. 6 **BEAR** Russia

No. 7 **LEOPARD** O.P.E.C.?

No. 8 **BEAST** U.N.S.C.

Revelation: Chapter 17
Vs. 1

"--Come, I will show you the judgement [destruction] of the great harlot [Mystery Babylon] that sitteth upon many waters.

As earlier noted, Scripture is implying in this text that the destruction of Mystery Babylon takes place between the fifth and sixth governments on Revelations list of eight Kingdoms.

When this statement is examined in light of the chart's profile of the "inner court", the evidence clearly points to Mystery Babylon's destruction occurring between the alliance of the lion/eagle governments and the bear. And, according to Scripture's outline in Revelation 18, it will be devastation that inaugurates a world-wide financial collapse.

Subsequently, many will believe that the hour has arrived for the Church to put on its finest dress in preparation for the Groom's coming for His bride. However, there is evidence that the Church may instead be required to put on her heaviest armor in preparation for a great spiritual battle.

As for the culmination of "beast" government and its conflict with the Church, Scripture has considerably more to add to these subjects in the following pages.

Chapter VI

The Beast and It's Image

Shadows of his Coming

Had this study included Scripture describing Christ's second coming, several chapters could be added to this report. It has instead focused on that volatile period before Christ's return, prophecy that concerns the city labeled Mystery Babylon, the beast government within it, and the coming antichrist. In keeping with this study's goal, the following pages will now examine Revelation 13, and how this controversial chapter relates to the above topics.

When explored, chapter 13 will reveal that it has woven within it, two subjects. The first describes the beast's infrastructure, the number of nations that control it and the deadly wound one of them receives. Also included in this segment are its three political divisions as Scripture describes them as part leopard, bear and lion.

The second theme is found in verses four through ten as Scripture now records how satan will influence the beast kingdom as a world order. Following this interruption, verse 11 continues with

Scripture's opening comments about the beast government, including recovery of the beast's deadly wound, restoration of its political power, and the introduction of the antichrist to the world.

Part Bear, Leopard and Lion

Using symbols to describe how the beast kingdom is constructed politically, the following verses profile this mysterious government, including the 17 nations that will control it:

Revelation: Chapter 13
Vs. 1

> And I stood upon the sand of the sea, and I saw a beast rise up out of the sea, having seven heads and ten horns, and upon his horns ten crowns, and upon his heads the name of blasphemy.

Vs. 2

> And the beast which I saw was like a leopard, and his feet were like the feet of a bear, and his mouth like the mouth of a lion; and the dragon gave him his power, and his throne and great authority.

As earlier noted, the beast described rising out of the sea in verse one is a government controlled by a 17-nation committee. According to this text, seven are delegates from nations it calls **"heads"**, and added to these seven are ten additional men from ten nations called **"horns"**.

In addition to the fact that Scripture states that the beast receives its authority to rule the earth directly from "the dragon" (satan), Scripture also implies that this alliance of 17 members is indirectly controlled by three separate systems of government. Interestingly, they are the same kingdoms (less the eagle) that the seventh chapter of Daniel also described.

According to this account in Revelation, some of the beast's members will represent the leopard federation. These nations, as previously noted, would probably come from the Moslem-dominated Middle East, and as a unified group would control over half the world's oil reserves. This alliance would also have the eight members to match the eight segments recorded in Daniel 7:6 (the four heads and four wings).

The second group within this political coalition is portrayed by the feet of the (Russian) bear. Its membership would not only represent the socialist governments, but as implied in verse two with its reference to the bear's claws, in the last days it becomes the source of military hardware to this world body.

Last to be included in this alliance are the democratic nations of the free world. However, due to Scripture's comment about the eagle, and its re-moval as a super power (Daniel 7:4), Revelation now depicts the lion as "standing" alone. It further implies, that as the "mouth" of the beast, the lion is the new host nation to this world government as well. It is from these three factions, the Moslem/

Arab alliance, Russia's new Commonwealth of Independent States (CIS) and the free democratic nations, that this eighth government called "The Beast" is derived. Scripture confirms this theory in the following verse as John details for the Church the fatal wound that brings down one of the important seven heads of the beast:

The Deadly Wound

Vs. 3

> **And I saw one of his heads as though it were wounded to death; and his deadly wound was healed, and all the world wondered after the beast.**

John states in verse three that after the beast government receives its deadly wound, **"all the world wondered after the beast."** In other words, he is saying that because of the immense influence of this one nation (or head), the world questioned what would be the outcome of the beast government without this one special nation supporting it.

In all probability the **"deadly"** wound to one of its heads is the result of the destruction of New York City and the subsequent down-fall of the United States; therefore two important points previously brought out are reexamined at this time. The first was found in Revelation 18 where Scripture warned the Church that this seaport city of the beast government is to be destroyed by a great fire.

The second point was found in Daniel 7:4. Here Scripture noted that an alliance would involve two kingdoms, one of them representing the wings of an eagle as they is "torn" from view, leaving the lion as the second kingdom to fend for itself. A statement that suggests there is some type of violence regarding the removal of the eagle from the world's political scene.

Should the UN Security Council be this dreaded government called the beast which has for one of its heads the United States, Revelation implies in verse three that there may be a deadly wound imposed upon this nation as its key supporter.

Subsequently, the previously outlined destruction of New York City would not only deliver a serious wound to the United Nations and its powerful Security Council, but it supports the comment in Revelation 13:3 that "**the world wondered**" if the beast could continue as a working government. This devastation would also render a crippling blow to a dept ridden economy within the United States, forcing the lion of Great Britain to fend for itself as previously noted by Daniel.

It is widely recognized that the United States is the backbone of the United Nations. And with the absence of this support, many would rightfully question if the UN could survive without it. A record of support that is not only political, but also to the extent that the United States is responsible for twenty five percent of the UN's total budget.

As noted earlier, there is a break in Revelation's description of the beast government beginning with verse four. To better understand Scripture's focus concerning the wound to this world government and its warning to the Church concerning its recovery, this study will bypass Scripture's comments on satan's influence within it. It will instead, go directly to verse 11 where the continuing description of the beast government unfolds, along with its introduction of the antichrist:

The Antichrist

Vs. 11

> **And I beheld another beast coming out of the earth; and he had two horns like a lamb** (with him), **and he spoke like a dragon.**

Vs. 12

> **And he exerciseth all the power of the first beast before him, and causeth the earth and them that dwell on it to worship the first beast, whose deadly wound was healed.**

In the opening verse of this chapter, John commented on the beast government and its deadly wound. Beginning with verse 11, John continues with his description of the beast and its recovery by introducing three new government representatives, one of which is the future antichrist (or his nation's representative) prior to his assuming power in this powerful bureaucracy.

It is also likely that the wound to the beast government in verse three involves the loss of life

134

to diplomates when the UN Building in New York is destroyed. A probability that could be directly tied to the deaths of the three horn members examined earlier in Daniel 7:8. As a result of Daniel's prophecy, all three of these men in verse 11 are now needed to complete the Security Council's ten member requirement.

With the UN Charter being a valid instrument of world power, the antichrist would be wise to take full advantage of it as Scripture suggests he will. According to verse 12, the antichrist is given the power and authority of **"the first beast."** This comment is important in that it is telling the Church that he does not initiate the beast government, but rather that he becomes affiliated with it after its near collapse in verse three.

Verse 12 also points to the fact that the antichrist does not ask that he should be worshiped, but that he instead **"causeth the earth and them who dwell on it to worship -- the first beast."** He asks the world to support a government already in operation.

Offering additional insight into this chapter is the term **"worship"**. As an expression, it does not in any way suggest the type of worship that one would offer at some altar or temple. It refers instead to the kind of adoration and devotion that one would hold for a favorite sports team or political organization.

An Oppressive Leader

Vs. 13

And he doeth great wonders, so that he maketh fire come down from heaven on the earth in the sight of men.

Vs. 14

And deceiveth them that dwell on the earth by those miracles which he had power to do in the sight of the beast, saying to them that dwell on the earth, that they should make an image to the beast, that had the wound by the sword, and did live.

Vs. 15

And he had power to give life unto the image of the beast, that the image of the beast should both speak, and cause that as many as would not worship the image of the beast should be killed.

As Daniel continues with his profile of the antichrist and his affiliation to the beast government, verse 13 suggests that as a tyrant, he has either previously demonstrated his ability to create world problems or he has proved he has the means at his command to do so in the future. Scripture also implies that after using his military expertise to fraudulently obtain leadership of this wounded government, the antichrist convinces the members

136

of the beast government that they should **"make an image to the** [previous] **beast -- that had the wound by the sword and did live."**

For centuries the Church has assumed that the **"image"** of the beast described in verse 15 is some kind of statue given the ability to speak. Contrary to this past theory, and considering all the evidence, the image of the wounded beast is not some statue or any resemblance of a person. It will instead be a new building to replace the present UN structure in New York City, which in all probability would be ruined or made inaccessible when Mystery Babylon is destroyed as outlined in Revelation 18. The proposed new structure will then serve as the seat of government and new home for both the United Nations and its influential 17-member Security Council.

In verse one of this chapter, the head or mouth of the end-time beast is described as the lion. Coincidentally, should a new UN Building as **"the image of the beast"** be rebuilt in Great Britain, it would be erected in the nation where the UN originally began operations. The UN became an official world organization in 1945, and relocated in New York City in the fall of 1952.

In the following verses, Revelation suggests that during this period of world reorganization, the antichrist's power and influence will be at its peak. According to this text, he boldly demands, under penalty of death, total allegiance from all the world to his revived beast government. He accomplishes this feat by tightening the controls of how the world's nations and their citizens can buy and sell:

The Mark of The Beast . . .

Vs. 16

And he causeth all, both small and great, rich and poor, free and slave, to receive a mark in their right hand, or in their foreheads.

Vs. 17

That no man might buy or sell, unless he had the mark, or the name of the beast, or the number of his name.

Due to the recent working history of the modern computer in the business world, it is probable that there has been a serious misinterpretation of verse 17. It is not so much that when this verse is closely examined, two types of codes or identification systems are outlined. Rather, it is that these two codes are directed at two totally different branches or accounts within this world government.

Verse 17 states that: "**no man can buy or sell unless he had the name or mark of the beast -- or the number of his name.**" It should be noted that this statement is not referring to the antichrist that Scripture addresses in the following eighteenth verse. It is instead describing two separate ledgers designed solely for the purpose of accounting, systems which could not be supported on a worldwide scale if not for the modern computer and its ability for storing financial transactions.

The first system this text describes is "the mark -- or name of the beast[s]." Up to this point, Scripture is addressing only the individual member nations of the beast government, not the population within them. It is a code name that will be given to each of the member nations to allow international trade to be successfully carried out between them. These nations, like those in the past, must trade with other countries in order for them to grow and prosper. "The mark or name of the beast" is a statement regarding the identity of these various nations. It also becomes a tool necessary to keep a running account of which nation has either a surplus trade balance, such as Japan, or is a debtor nation, as the United States.

The second code in verse 17 is a numbering sequence referring to "the number of his [or her] name." It is not the number 666, as the following verse has led many to believe (and would have very little numerical value for accounting purposes). Rather, it speaks instead to the individual and their personal identification number in order for them to make purchases within that country where they are citizens. A social security or tax number would be more then adequate for this purpose. Under such a plan, commerce would not only be carried out successfully within that nation, but the need for large amounts of capital would also be eliminated.

In either the case of the name or code of a trading nation, or the numbering of its citizens, those in control of such a program could demand total political support before issuing either system.

Believing that New York City along with the present UN building will be destroyed, the United

States as an economic community would be left in complete ruin. It would also force the world to find a new source for financial stability between trading nations. This fact is verified in Revelation 18:11 where it states that immediately after Mystery Babylon's destruction, "the merchants of the world wept; for no man buyeth their merchandise any more."

The two previously mentioned accounts could be the answer for such a worldwide economic disaster, because all it would require is a computer to assist and control international banking. A simple ledger listing nations with their debits or surpluses, thereby setting the world's economy back on the road to recovery.

The failure of the Church to separate "**the mark, or name of the beast**" from "**the number of his name,**" has underscored the fact that it has not fully understood the extent of the financial problems of the last days. The Church is also not prepared that it will be obligated to participate in this world effort to stabilize a very seriously crippled economy.

It will be support that becomes a conflict for many within the Church, not in being assigned a specific account number, but being ordered to impregnate this number on their persons, mainly on the backs of their hands or on their foreheads.

The Number "666"

Concluding this study chapter is a riddle as to how the Church, by closely examining the beast government, can identify not only the antichrist, but also the time of his arrival:

Vs. 18

Here is wisdom, let him that has understanding count the number of the beast [government]; **for it is the number of a man; and his number is six hundred and sixty-six.**

At first glance, this verse when read by itself may appear difficult to solve or interpret; however, every government and major institution (including most churches), have kept a running account of how many leaders they have had over their histories. For example, British Royalty has from the start of its eleven hundred years of existence, recorded 62 Monarchs up to Queen Elizabeth II. President Reagan was the fortieth President of the United States just as John F. Kennedy was the thirty-fifth. Pope John Paul II, the former Cardinal Karol Wojtyla of Poland, is the 266 successor to Saint Peter as the spiritual leader of the Roman Catholic Church.

Consequently, the most important clue in finding the needed answer to this age-old question regarding the number 666 and its affiliation to the antichrist may be found in one of the rules under which the Security Council operates. As previously noted, due to the immense power of the council, the office of its president is held for only one month at a time, rotating alphabetically between both its permanent and temporary member nations.

Surprising as it may be to some, Scripture is informing the Church in verse 18 that if it counts the number of the beast government (the Security Council) by counting its past presidents, it will identify the antichrist as the 666 person on the list. If then, one counts the total number of months this body of members has existed as a working coalition, an interesting fact comes into focus -- the number of its presidents who have governed it during its brief lifetime.

In numbering the presidents of the Security Council from the date of their first official meeting in January 1946, count no fewer than 12 presidents serving it in any given year. However, due to a member not able to complete his term in office, some months may have had more than one president. In either situation, the 666 president of the Security Council takes control of this world body no later then the year 2001.

The graph on p.143 will better explain how these dates and totals fall in line with recent history, especially in light of Israel's becoming a nation again as shown on the calendar beneath it.

The top portion of the graph numbers the UN Security Council presidents beginning with its first chairman, January 1946. It also reveals the "666" president who, as the possible antichrist, must take office at his appointed month.

142

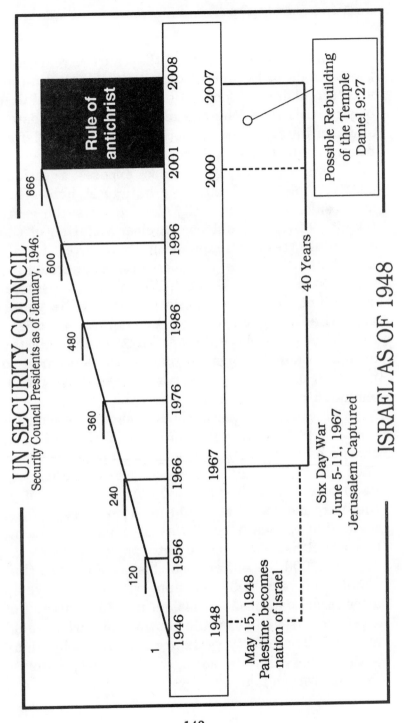

UN SECURITY COUNCIL
Security Council Presidents as of January, 1946.

666

600

480

360

240

120

1

1946 1956 1966 1976 1986 1996 2001 2008

Rule of antichrist

1948 1967 2000 2007

May 15, 1948
Palestine becomes
nation of Israel

Six Day War
June 5-11, 1967
Jerusalem Captured

40 Years

Possible Rebuilding
of the Temple
Daniel 9:27

ISRAEL AS OF 1948

143

The bottom portion of the chart reveals how these totals of Security Council Presidents line up with the history of modern-day Israel. A record that begins with 1948 (the end of the British Mandate), and continues to the fortieth anniversary of Israel taking control of Jerusalem (1967-2007).

This two-part graph also exposes a serious charter violation. Should the antichrist hold office as president of the Security Council for seven years (Daniel 9:27), he would be in clear violation of the one-month term stipulated in its charter for its presidents. Scripture, however, may have accounted for this violation in Daniel 7:25. In this text Daniel states that **"he** [the antichrist] **changes the times and the laws; and they are given into his hand."** A possible reference to a change in the Security Council's bylaws enabling the antichrist to maintain control over this government body for an extended period of time.

There is another fact that should be considered. When the seven years the antichrist will be in charge of world affairs are added on to the year 2001, the 666 president of the Security Council will be in power into the year 2008. As earlier noted, if there are months that would need an early replacement due to death or illness of a past president, the antichrist could come into power as early as 1999 or 2000. In either case this would mean that about the year 2007, or approximately 40 years after Israel captured Jerusalem in 1967, the end of a proposed seven-year rule by the antichrist would also end. These forty years are recognized by many within the Church as a possible requisite to Christ's return.

144

Summary: Revelation Chapter 13

When one examines the dominant governments within the United Nations, three powerful political categorizes will emerge, the most prominent being the United States and Great Britain, who between them, represent the free world. In addition to this democratic representation is the nation of Russia, and despite the release of its satellite nations, it still has strong socialistic tendencies and is militarily very powerful. This leaves the third and last power within the coalition, the oil-rich Middle East.

The control of the UN by these three super-powers is due in part not because of their wisdom or experience in world affairs, but because of their political influence. For this reason Revelation 13:2 states that the beast government will be indirectly comprised of three separate beasts or systems of governments -- the lion, the bear and the leopard. Three political systems of government that have little in common with each other, except their fear of the other, and that any one of the three can upset the delicate balance of world power.

It is to this fragile alliance of nations and their possible collapse which Revelation 13:3 refers. John records here that the beast government gains the attention of the entire world when one of its seven heads is severely wounded. It is a wound that

Revelation 18 described as greatly affecting both the world's commercial and political structure.

During this time of political uncertainty and financial crisis, the leaders of the world become an easy prey for the antichrist. Scripture clearly states in Revelation 13, that he fraudulently acquires their support. This could be achieved by the antichrist threatening some kind of military action, especially if he has acquired nuclear capabilities.

Scripture not only gave this man's identity as an Assyrian (modern-day Iraq) in Micah's 5:5-6, but Scripture may also have given the time of his arrival. Revelation 13:18 stated that the antichrist will be the 666 person on a numbering system within the beast government. With the present UN Security Council Charter calling for its presidents not to exceed a term of more then one month in office, the 666 president will take his chair as head of the Security Council on or just before 2001. And, as previously noted, the fact that he is able to change the laws may account for his being able to extend his one-month term as its president.

Should the UN Security Council be the beast government, the most interesting facet about the antichrist's term in office is that it will end at a date approximately 40 years after Israel began its occupation of Jerusalem. To those who study numerology, this fact is meaningful as there has never been a spiritual event in Scripture without the number are preceding it. Supporting this comment are some of the events beginning with the number 40 in Scripture:

Noah and the flood: Genesis 7:17
Giving of the law: Exodus 24:18
David and Goliath: 1st Samuel 17:16
Christ's ministry: Matthew 4:2

Another 40 that could be included in this list involves Israel before her becoming a nation for the first time. Beginning in Numbers 13:25, through to 14:33, Scripture records the 40 days the Jews spied out the land of Canaan, which was then followed by the 40 years of wandering in the desert. Equally important are the forties that followed Christ's death in 30 A.D. The first was the 40 days of Christ's reappearance to the disciples in Acts 1:3. The second is the Temple's destruction forty years later in 70 A.D. These last two forties proved to be the critical in that they marked the beginning of the present Church age.

As an added example of how the number 40 is related to most scriptural events the Church has long believed that humankind is the only creation of God conceived with a soul and spirit. With this fact in mind, this study should include the gestation period of an infant within its mother's womb, the interim of 40 weeks from conception to birth.

Believing that the previous examples all point to the twentieth century as that critical period for revealing the antichrist and the beast government to the Church, it is likely that both exist at this present time.

If then, the twentieth century is that generation, does Scripture offer to the Church other recognizable facts to further substantiate the theory of the beast government being the Security Council?

147

This question is answered in the closing pages of this study as the remaining portion of Micah's fifth chapter is examined.

Chapter Vll

"Seven Shepherds and Eight Principal Men"

Shadows of his Coming

Building on the assumption that Scripture's mention of the beast government with its seven heads and ten horns is none-other than the UN Security Council, and that the antichrist will emerge from this world body, the following pages will now examine the concluding verses of Micah's fifth chapter.

In the opening pages of this report, Micah's fourth chapter began with his describing the pain of Israel's struggle for renewed statehood and the bitter fighting that would follow. Micah's central message, however, is not the record of Israel's recent history, but its implied reference to the return and reign of Christ which must soon follow these events.

A reading of Micah's fourth chapter along with the first three verses of chapter five noted that a military siege will come upon Israel from the future antichrist. This was a prophecy that Micah 4:8 suggested would take place within one generation of Israel's rebirth as a nation.

Continuing now with Micah's comments about this special generation, the opening verses of chapter five are reviewed, beginning with the misplaced reference about Israel's invasion by the antichrist:

Vs. 1

Now gather thyself in troops, O daughter of troops -- he [the antichrist] **has laid siege against us --**

As earlier noted, this brief statement describing a military battle against Israel was incorrectly positioned by translators as belonging to verse one of chapter five. This portion of Scripture should have been the closing comment to chapter four and Micah's prophecy about Israel's problems as a new nation. An encounter that concludes with the coming of the antichrist, and his invasion of Israel as the last event in her struggle for survival.

This assertion is supported in the balance of verse one and the following two verses. In this text, the focus of chapter five changes as Micah records in reversed order, statements about the Messiah's birth and His rejection by the Jewish community. Micah continues in verse three by adding that it would be Israel's rejection of their Messiah that becomes the principle cause for God terminating them as a nation (70-130 A.D.):

Vs. 1b

They shall smite [Christ,] **the judge of Israel with a rod upon the cheek.**

150

Vs. 2

But thou, Bethlehem Ephrathah, though thou be little among the thousands of Judah, yet out of thee shall He come forth unto Me that is to be ruler in Israel, whose goings forth have been from of old, and everlasting --

Vs. 3

Therefore will He give them up -- until the time that she who travaileth has brought forth -- then the remnant of his brethren shall return unto the children of Israel.

These two-and-a-half verses are typical of prophetic Scripture which is not written in the order of events. Micah begins this inverted statement with a short reference to Christ's suffering and death in verse one, and then he continues in verse two by naming Bethlehem as the city of Christ's birth.

Scripture's use of these reversed comments was never intended to obstruct its focus concerning Israel's glorious future. It was instead introduced as a tool to understand Micah's message of Israel's rebirth and Christ's return.

This becomes apparent as Scripture explains in verse three that the rejection of the Messiah as foretold in verses one and two would one day be the principle cause for Israel being dismantled as a nation. This prophecy became a reality for the Jewish people some forty years after Christ's death.

151

The statement in verse three: **"Therefore shall He give them up,"** not only supports the prophecy Micah made earlier in the previous two verses about the Jewish people and the implied rejection of Christ, but Micah also adds a crucial comment in verse three that relates to chapter four: **"Therefore will He give them up--until--."**

The crux of this statement is Micah's addition of the word **"until"**. Besides Israel being chastened for their rejection of Christ, a twofold promise of hope is attached to this reprimand. Both directly relating to verse ten of Micah's fourth chapter. This statement is supported beginning with the following two disclosures:

First, the Jewish exile from Israel will continue **"until --** [or, ends with] **the time when she who travaileth has brought forth** [as a nation again]." This prophecy was followed by Micah's second prediction: **"then the remnant of His brethren shall return unto the children of Israel."** Both of these promises were fulfilled beginning on November 30, 1947, when in New York City, a special Jewish remnant witnessed their petition for a second Israel approved by the United Nations, legally allowing them to return to the land of their ancestors the following spring, May 15, 1948.

The comments in verse three about Israel becoming a nation again and a Jewish remnant being allowed to return to it, are in direct reference to Micah's fourth chapter. In verse ten, Micah not only describes that generation as a "woman in travail," but he also labels the city of Israel's rebirth as "Babylon". As previously noted, this comment has grave consequences when included as part of Micah's prophecy about Israel's rebirth.

In addition to these two prophecies, Micah adds a third promise in the following fourth verse as he foretells of the Messiah's reign during Israel's second tenure as a nation:

Vs. 4

And He shall stand and feed His flock in the strength of the Lord, in the majesty of the name of the Lord, His God, and they [Israel] **shall dwell secure, for then shall He** [the risen Christ] **be great even to the ends of the earth.** (Amplified Version)

Scripture's Signal of Christ's Return

Supporting Micah's comments in verse four regarding the Messiah's coming reign is the following verse. In this text Micah makes a comment about how the Church can identify this critical time, its association with Christ's return and the key component that will usher it into being:

Vs. 5a

And this shall be the peace, when the Assyrian shall come into our land -- and when he shall tread in our palaces.

At first glance verse five (5a) implies that peace will come to Israel with the introduction of an Assyrian. When fully examined, however, verse five

153

reveals instead a warning to the Church about the coming antichrist and should be read as follows:

"**And this shall be the** [signal of when this] **peace** [in verse Four will come to the world,] **when the Assyrian shall come into our land** [Israel]; **and when he shall tread in our palaces.**"

Scripture implies here that shortly after Israel becomes a nation for a second time and has gone through the pain and suffering described in Micah's fourth chapter, an Assyrian (from modern-day Iraq) will come into power. And following his introduction to the world, his goal will be to eradicate the new nation of Israel. This invasion will be the sign or signal of Christ's soon return, an encounter that Scripture further describes in the following verses, and one that the Church may be unprepared to hear:

Agents of Liberation

Vs. 5b
Then shall we raise against him seven shepherds, and eight principal men.

Micah makes a statement in this text that until recently, would be very difficult to identify. He records in verse five that 15 men will wage a counter attack against the antichrist after his siege of Israel. However, Micah has broken them into two distinctive groups: **"Seven shepherds -- and eight principal men."**

These 15 men and how they break down is very important to this study. And when examined, add validity to the theory that the UN Security Council is the end-time beast government.

In previous pages, the composition of the beast government was given as follows: Seven heads (men in charge), with ten additional support members making a total of 17 participants. But in verse five, only 15 men are accounted for, two short of this government's 17 member requirement.

Micah's seven shepherds account for the seven heads or permanent members of the UN Security Council, but his reference to eight principal men leaves two people missing when aligned with the councils ten alternating members. However, when all the facts are examined, there is a valid reason for this difference as Scripture reveals two additional men, one of which it identified as one of the missing horn members.

This world figure was previously introduced in the earlier study of Daniel's seventh chapter. Daniel recorded in verse 24 that the antichrist emerges into the forefront of world politics from that division within the beast government called the ten horns.

As for the tenth horn or last needed **"principal"** member, Revelation 19:20 and 20:10 may hold the answer regarding this question. Both verses record that after Christ returns, two important men are cast into hell:

Revelation 19:
Vs. 20

> And the beast [the antichrist who controls it] was taken along with the false prophet that wrought miracles before him by which he deceived them that had received the mark of the beast, and them that worshiped his image. These both were cast alive into a lake of burning with brimstone.

Revelation 20:
Vs. 10

> And the devil that deceived them was cast into the lake of fire and brimstone, where the beast [the antichrist] and the false prophet are, and they shall be tormented day and night for ever and ever.

As for the possibility of the false prophet coming out of the UN, many tend to associate the title of "**prophet**" with one's ability to predict the future. This term, however, can be given to anyone who boasts that a particular event will go in his or her favor, such as an athletic couch or military advisor. It is the last example that will now be examined in light of facts given in Scripture as it implies that the false prophet is somehow involved with the military.

According to Revelation 19:20, the false prophet will deceive many by manipulating the beast government with his use of "**miracles**". A statement that is also suggested in Revelation 13:13-14 where

Scripture tells of the antichrist's ability to do much the same, but with additional details:

Revelation 13:
Vs. 13
> **And he [the antichrist] doeth great wonders, so that he maketh fire come down from the heaven on the earth in the sight of men.**

Vs. 14
> **And deceiveth them that dwell on the earth by those miracles which he had power to do in the sight of the beast. . .**

Should the so called miracles the false prophet is involved with in Revelation 19:20, be the same miracles as recorded in chapter 13:13-14, the implication may be some military action. Scripture's comment about fire coming down from heaven is probably modern weaponry such as a scud missile or some sophisticated successor to it. In either case, the reference to incoming fire is an important statement because it would be near impossible for the antichrist or his prophet advisor to gain world power without some kind of military capabilities.

According to these two Scriptures, should the false prophet also be a part of the beast government, Scripture will then have fully accounted for all 17 men of the UN Security Council as shown in the following chart.

— THE UN SECURITY COUNCIL —
Permanent Members / Official Languages

1. G.B. = English
2. U.S.A. = English
3. Russia = Russian
4. China = Chinese
5. France = French
6. _____ = Arabic
7. _____ = Spanish

— TEN SHORT TERM MEMBERS —
Replaced every two years from
within UN General Assembly

1._____
2._____
3._____
4._____
5._____
6. _____
7. _____
8. _____
9. Antichrist
10. False Prophet ?

Supporting the charts similarity to Revelation's outline of the beast government is Micah's comment in verse 5b. In this text, Micah foretells of 15 men coming to the aid of Israel when under the siege of the antichrist. A statement that may also explain the previously examined pardon in Daniel's seventh chapter:

Daniel 7:
Vs. 12

> **As for the rest of the beasts** [representatives], **they had their dominion taken away -- yet their lives were prolonged for a season and a time.**

Daniel implies here that after Christ's return, several world leaders associated with the beast government are allowed to live after they surrender their authority to the Church.

It is very probable that the pardon recorded in Daniel is in reference to Micah's next verse. In this text, Micah describes 15 prominent men as they come to the aid of Israel after the invasion by the antichrist:

Israel's Last Battle

Vs. 6

> **And they** [the seven shepherds and eight principal men] **shall smite the land of Assyria with the sword, and the land of Nimrod in the entrances of it; thus shall He** [Christ] **deliver us from the Assyrian, when he** [the antichrist] **comes into our land, and when he treadeth within our borders.**

Not only does Micah mention for the third time that the antichrist will come out of the ancient land of Assyria, he also states that "**they**", the seven shepherds and eight principal men of verse five, come against the antichrist in **"the land of Nimrod."**

The map on p.161 will show this area as being a fertile valley inside Iraq between the Euphrates and Tigris Rivers so named because of a series of four cities founded in this valley by Nimrod. According to Genesis 10:8-10, these were the cities of Babel, Erech, Accade and Calneh, located in the plains of Shinar.

As for the outcome of this conflict, Scripture promises victory for Israel in verse six as it adds the phrase **"Thus shall He** [the Messiah] **deliver us from the Assyrian -- when he** [the antichrist] **comes into our land."** This text implies that when Israel is rescued from the antichrist, God will use these 15 men as His principal tool for this gruesome task.

They are the same 15 men who, in delivering Israel from the occupation of the antichrist, carry the war into his own land; **"They shall smite the land of Assyria with the sword."** Again, this statement implicates modern-day Iraq as having a vital role in the battle of Armageddon.

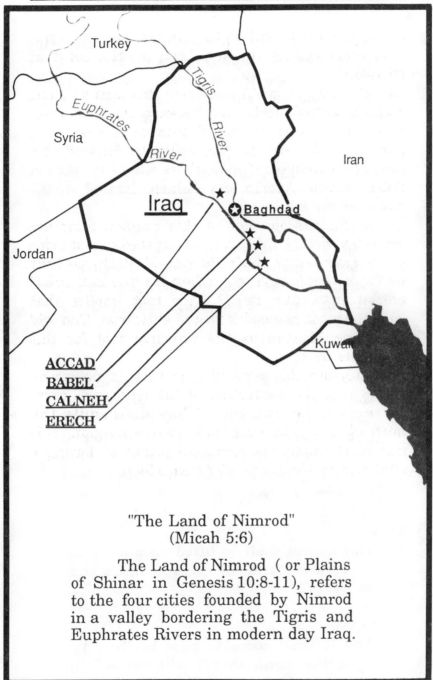

"The Land of Nimrod"
(Micah 5:6)

The Land of Nimrod (or Plains
of Shinar in Genesis 10:8-11), refers
to the four cities founded by Nimrod
in a valley bordering the Tigris and
Euphrates Rivers in modern day Iraq.

As Micah concludes this chapter, the following verses describe two concerns that could involve the Church. They are the survival of Jewish people escaping from the antichrist, and their spiritual focus during this dark hour of testing:

Worldwide Tribulation

Vs. 7

And the remnant of Jacob shall be in the midst of many people like due from the Lord, like the showers upon the grass, that tarrieth not for man, nor waiteth for the sons of men.

Vs. 8

And the remnant of Jacob shall be among the nations in the midst of many people, like a lion among the beast of the forest, like a young lion among the flocks of sheep, who, if he goes through, both treadeth down, and teareth in pieces, and none can deliver.

Vs. 9

Thine hand shall be lifted up upon thine adversaries, and all thine enemies shall be cut off.

Vs. 10

And it shall come to pass in that day, saith the Lord, that I will cut off thy horses out of the midst of thee, and I will destroy thy chariots;

Vs. 11

And I will cut off the cities of thy land, and throw down all thy strongholds;

Vs. 12

And I will cut off witchcrafts out of thine hand, and thou shalt have no soothsayers;

Vs. 13

Thy carved images also will I cut off, and thy standing images out of the midst of thee; and thou shalt no more worship the work of thine hands.

Vs. 14

And I will pluck up thine idols out of the midst of thee; so will I destroy thy cities.

Vs. 15

And I will execute vengeance in anger and fury upon the nations, such as they have never heard.

As Micah comments again about "that day", he indirectly points to his prophecy about Israel's rebirth and the return of Christ in chapter four. It should be noted that these verses speak of judgment. And it can be assumed that they are addressing both the Church and the Jewish remnant regarding the subject of idols. Micah describes the tearing down of several of them, all described as works of the hands. And although the term "idols" is used, it could also be applied to those many possessions and areas in one's life that have become masters instead of remaining servants.

In a statement to the Church about the last days, Micah concludes this chapter with a warning that the world will be as no other time in history. The judgment and hostility mentioned in verse 15 refers to the Battle of Armageddon and the great loss of life it will bring. Although Micah does not describe this conflict as vividly as Ezekiel or Zechariah, his comments are still worth noting, for it is in these two chapters that God gives needed details found in no other book within Scripture.

Summary: Micah Chapter 5

From the time of Christ's death, a favorite pastime of the Church has been its attempt to identify the personage of the antichrist. A guessing game that over the decades has mislead the Church from Nero to Adolf Hitler. Throughout this period of searching, however, several clues recorded in Micah's record remained uncovered. Among them was critical information that could only be correctly identified after Israel would again be established as a nation.

As this study draws to a close, it acknowledges that neither Micah's fourth nor fifth chapters have been very popular as prophetic reading. Yet it is a fact that Micah has a great amount of information to give the end-time Church regarding the subject of Israel's rebirth and Christ's return.

Assuming Micah's fourth chapter and his description of Israel's rebirth and her successive victories are legitimate prophecies for the twentieth century, it would be prudent to regard Micah's fifth chapter and his comments about the antichrist as also being valid. Given these facts, one should carefully examine Micah's statements regarding the antichrist who will assail Israel in the last days and his remarks that this invader will be coming from modern day Iraq.

Micah also described a military coup, an event that is as old as history itself. In his account, 15 individuals are mentioned, seven of whom he describes as shepherds (or leaders) and the balance as eight principal men. According to verse five, God will use these 15 men as His tool to remove the antichrist from power. And in doing so, He may also fulfill an important Old Testament prophecy:

Ezekiel 38:
Vs. 21

> "For I will call for a sword against him [the antichrist] throughout all my mountains, [or nations] saith the Lord God -- Every man's sword shall be against his brother."

Considering the power of the UN Security Council and its unique membership structure, it is probable that the seven shepherds and eight principal men come from this important body.

Chapter VIII

Babylon's Judgment, Its Cause and Effect

Shadows of his Coming

Believing that the media is often used to accomplish God's purpose, the NBC television talk show "Meet the Press," had as their guest in early January, 1989, well-known British-American author, journalist, and historian, Alistair Cooke. In the discussion about his writings on America, Mr. Cooke made an interesting comment about New York City, calling it "the world's third Babylon."

Also introduced in that same year was a miniseries called "the Eagle and the Bear." (cable TV, AEN). Their promotion heralded it as "a riveting series about the global tug-of-war between the United States and Russia."

It is entirely possible that while the Church remained unaware of the inner court's importance to prophecy and of its direct correlation to Daniel's prediction for the twentieth century, the media not only identified two of its symbols, they also recognized the basic similarities between New York City and Babylon of old.

Despite these two examples, some still contend that the historic city of Rome, the world's second Babylon, the only heir apparent and candidate for this city. Strengthening their position that it would be unlikely that Mystery Babylon would be an integral part of the United States, many point to the fact that when the New Testament was recorded in the first century, Rome, the sin capital of that period, was referred to as Babylon by the Apostle Peter (1 Peter 5:13). It should be noted, however, that the Church was also expecting Christ to return at that time.

A Nation In Need of Revival

Aside from their misgivings that New York City could be involved in prophecy, most of these same people would readily concede that the Twentieth Century Church has witnessed dramatic changes in the lifestyle of the United States. This is especially noticed in the court's recent decisions in areas where Christian values are concerned. One of which defined the U.S. Constitution to imply that conveying Scripture or prayer in public schools is contrary to the nation's best interests. Then, to further offend the Church, legislators openly encourage the schools to distribute condoms and birth control advice to students of all ages.

Supporting this study's position that New York City is Mystery Babylon, and that the U.S. is due to have its (eagle's) wings clipped, is Micah's prophecy that one generation will witness both

Israel's rebirth as a nation and Christ's return. Nonetheless, this report acknowledges that it will be difficult for some to accept the results of this study, for many are firmly entrenched in the belief that the United States is too God-fearing as a nation to possess this notorious city.

As for those who doubt that the United States deserves God's correction, the crime statistics readily show otherwise. Independent studies reveal that as a nation it is sinking into immorality more then can be tolerated if it is to continue as a functioning society.

Compounding this decline is the government's tax policy on the working family, especially those with children. Most homes must now have both parents in the work force. This reality has caused serious damage to this nation's family structure and contributes greatly to the divorce rate. And except for a few legislators who see a serious need for changing the tax laws on this over taxed group, most have forced the working family to be more concerned with their financial survival than with advancing any spiritual commitment.

It is true that the United States offers much in the way of personal opportunities to enhance one's lifestyle. However, aside from their spiritual aspect, most of these freedoms are superficial and often deceiving, even to the Church. Many Christians now spend more time in their TV Guide than in their Bibles. And if not watching some entertaining event, they prefer instead to read the latest on some sporting achievement or financial investment.

Because of this outward success, many within the Church have misconstrued God's patience with the United States as being His approval, and assume that it will continue. Nothing strays further from the truth than this false assumption. To those who doubt this counsel, the following is an example of God's punishment to a nation that willfully turns away from Him. A warning of judgment to Old Testament Israel that could easily be directed to the United States:

Jeremiah 45:
Vs. 5

> "Behold that which I have built I will break down, and that which I have planted I will pluck up -- even this whole land."

Assuming the Lord loves these United States, as He did ancient Israel, would it not be unwise then to expect some disciplinary action from Him as well? This facet of God's character is also verified in the following verse:

Proverbs 3:
Vs. 12

> "For whom the Lord loves -- He corrects, even as a father corrects the son in whom he delights." (Amplified Version)

This "correction" of love could be easily achieved, for aside from the fact that the stability of the United States dollar is chiefly derived from investments generated on Wall Street, New York has in its control, the assets of nations abroad as well. Consequently, this city's destruction would not only bankrupt the United States, but would easily paralyze the rest of the world.

Along with the collapse of the U.S. dollar, the destruction of New York City would open the door for other prophecy to be considered at this time, beginning with world leaders coming together in an effort to bring back into society some representation of financial and civil order.

Currently there is only one working government body at this time to be called upon to solve such a global challenge, that being the United Nations and its powerful Security Council as recently demonstrated in many of the UN's peacekeeping resolutions.

Regarding the future of the United Nations, Scripture makes it clear that when Mystery Babylon receives its judgment, it not only destroys the financial underpinning of the world, it also destroys the throne or home of the beast government that is a vital part of this city as well. This would mean that New York City, along with its financial district, and the present United Nations Building, would all three be destroyed to accomplish the worldwide chaos as detailed in Scripture.

The Wounded Eagle

Believing New York City ("the big apple") is as rotten to the core as described in Revelation's profile of Mystery Babylon, it is this study's opinion that the next major event to take place within prophecy is this city's judgment. Drawing from

Scripture's outline in the previous pages, the destruction of New York City and the existing United Nations building would then open the door for the following Scriptural events to be fulfilled:

First, the destruction of New York City would result in the collapse of the American dollar, thus tumbling the U.S. "eagle" from its perch high over the world's list of superpowers (Daniel 7:4). And, due to the dollar underpinning the rest of the world's economy, the loss of this city would spawn a global recession unlike any other before it (Revelation 18:11).

Along with the collapse of the dollar and the U.S. losing its place as a world super power, Russia's acutely needed assistance from the western industrialized nations would also cease. This suspension of aid would not only curtail Russia's democratic endeavors, but it could easily be the cause for the bear to revert to its former policy of militancy as implied in Daniel 7:5:

Vs. 5

And behold another beast, a second, like to a bear, and it raised itself up on one side, and it had three ribs in the mouth of it, and they said thus unto it, Arise, devour much flesh.

Difficult as it is to accept at this time, considering the present situation in Russia, Daniel warns the Church that the bear will succeed the lion/eagle alliance as the world's sixth dominant power. The bear is then followed by an eight member alliance Daniel describes as a "leopard":

Vs. 6

After this I beheld another like a leopard, which had upon its back four wings of a fowl, the beast also had four heads; and dominion was given to it.

Revelation 17:10 further illuminates this passage by claiming that the seventh kingdom is in control for only a brief period. The Leopard kingdom is then succeeded by a government, "that was, and is not, and is the eighth, and is [made-up] of the [previous] seven [kingdoms of the inner court]." Revelation 13:2 supports this verse by contending that this last kingdom is comprised of the three political systems of government prominent in its day: the Moslem **Leopard**, the Democratic **Lion** and the Socialist **Bear**.

Again, the UN Security Council best fits this Scriptural outline as the most likely contender to be the dreaded eighth government. And as already mentioned, this government not only embraces all of the previous seven kingdoms and their territories controlled over the centuries, but the entire UN membership represents the three disclosed power structures, the up-and-coming Arab alliance -- the democratic nations -- and the socialist bloc.

According to the outline in Revelation 13:1-4, should New York City be destroyed, its destruction will temporarily leave the United Nations without a base for its operations. Interestingly, verse three implies that the UN and its Security Council continue to function as a governing body as this text records that the world closely watches the beast government during this critical period:

Vs. 3

> **And I saw one of his heads as [if] it were wounded to death; and his deadly wound was healed, and all the world wondered after the beast.**

The probable cause for this global attention toward the wounded beast is the severity of the worldwide fiscal crises, and the desperate need for some responsible government to solve the resulting international problems.

Also, the theory that the Security Council is active during this period was supported in the earlier study of Revelation 13:11. That study noted that, following the deadly wound to the beast, the antichrist (or his nation's representative) and two additional men are introduced as members of this important government body at this time:

Three Prophetic Appointments

Vs. 11

> **And I beheld another beast** [or government representative] **coming out of the earth; and he had** [with him] **two** [additional] **horns like a lamb, and he spoke like a dragon.**

Due to the deaths of the three horn members recorded in Daniel 7:8, the ten member requirement of the Security Council Charter is again complete with the addition of these three new representatives. And, according to the following verses, once the antichrist has representation on the Security Council, he attains power by means of some kind of military deception:

Vs. 12

And he exercised all the power of the first beast before him, and caused the earth and them which dwell therein to worship the first beast, whose deadly wound was healed.

Vs. 13

And he doeth great wonders, so that he maketh fire to come down from heaven on earth in the sight of men.

Vs. 14

And deceiveth them that dwell on the earth by those miracles which he had power to do in the sight of the beast; saying to them that dwell on the earth, that they should make an image to the beast, which had the wound by a sword, and did live.

Vs. 15

And he had power to give life unto the image of the beast, that the image of the beast should both speak, and cause as many that would not worship the beast should be killed.

It is also here that the fourth event in this series may unfold. Revelation implies in this text that the antichrist embarks on a program to construct a new United Nations building, replacing the previous structure destroyed along with New York City. The antichrist is quoted in verse 14 petitioning the members of the UN **"that they should make an image to the beast,"** complete with all of its former authority.

With the antichrist gaining power within the world's political community and the Security Council surpassing its former prestige, the next event to unfold may be a plan to solve the world's mounting financial problems due to the loss of the American dollar. Scripture adds in this text that during the reign of the antichrist, a worldwide plan of finance is introduced. And according to verse 17, the antichrist will enact into law a duel system of banking consisting of two divisions:

Vs. 17
"The mark or name of the beast[s] -- or -- the number of his [or her] name."

According to this verse, one of the possible concerns of the Security Council would be international trade. A system that would allow world governments to again have a credit line between themselves as trading partners; the second would be designed to use between individual nations and the citizens within them.

The first reference: **"The mark, or name of the** [individual] **beast** [government]," refers to the identification of specific nations so that trade can be carried out between them. This method of accounting is presently used and has been proven successful within the business community of many industrialized nations.

For personal purchases, however, a second system similar to a Social Security or tax number is described. Scripture refers to this second ledger as **"the number of his** [or her] **name."** This statement translates to be an identification number given all persons within their own nation in order for their government to keep record of their individual bank accounts.

According to Revelation 13:16, the numbering, or marking of individuals, is then applied to the hand or the forehead of each person. The result is a system for keeping track of individuals and their finances. It should also be mentioned that this executive order brings the Church into the forefront of a serious political problem due to the many within the Church who will refuse to pledge their allegiance to this new system.

The Rebuilt Temple

Following reconstruction of the world's financial community, the most critical event to occur during the antichrist's rule could evolve from Israel's effort to rebuild Jerusalem's Temple. This is verified in II Thessalonians 2:4. According to this text, the Temple's rebuilding will have a major role within this framework of political chaos and world uncertainty. Paul records that after the antichrist in-

vades Israel, he will use their new Temple as a
backdrop to announce to the world that he has
proven himself above all his enemies, including
Israel's God:

Vs. 4

**Who opposes and exalts himself above
every so-called god or object of worship,
so that he takes his seat in the Temple of
God, displaying himself as being God.**
(NAS)

Before this century and Israel's access to the
temple site (1967), it was believed that the original
Temple to have been under the Dome of the Rock.
Now, however, a number of Jewish scholars believe
it is just north of this Moslem holy sight under a
building called the "Dome of the Spirits." Like the
Dome of the Rock, the Dome of the Spirits is also
considered a religious structure, but it is not as
holy to the Moslems as the previous site.

This fact could be instrumental in solving a
serious problem in this war-torn area of the Middle
East because access to this site could easily open
the door for meaningful dialogue between Israel and
the Palestinians. Scripture supports this theory in
Daniel 9:27 where it states that there is some kind
of arrangement that involves Israel, the antichrist
and others concerning the Jewish Temple:

Vs. 27

**And he shall confirm a covenant with
many for one seven** (seven years)**; in the
middle of the seven he will put an end to**

sacrifice and offering. And on a wing of
the temple, he will set up an abomination
that causes desolation, until the end that
is decreed is poured out on him. (N.I.V.)

According to this Scripture, the antichrist "confirms" or approves of an agreement with "many",
possibly between the UN and the Palestinians,
allowing Israel to rebuild their Temple. It is obvious, however, should the Temple's original site be
part of this agreement, Israel would be required to
give something back in exchange for this treasured
possession.

As a further example of how Daniel's prophecy
might be fulfilled, the antichrist, as head of the UN
Security Council, could approve of such a treaty between Israel and the Palestinians. A UN agreement
would allow Israel the right to rebuild their Temple
on its original site in exchange for some conquered
Israeli territory designated as a Palestinian homeland.

This is only an example, but one that is valid
because it would have support within Israel's
religious right wing and her Likud Party, both of
whom previously said that they would never give
up any land for peace. Trading territory for the
Temple site, however, could be a totally different
matter, especially when one considers how these
two powerful groups have looked forward to Israel
again having a Temple with all its resulting identity. This action would also win the support of
Israel's Labor Party, a strong political division
within Israel that have long promoted the idea of
giving up some of its captured territory for a

Palestinian homeland, assuming it will bring peace to their troubled land.

Nonetheless, Daniel 9:24 makes it clear that problems arise three and a half years later, or about the length of time needed to relocate the existing Moslem structure, unearth the Temple's original foundation, and construct this long awaited place of worship. It is at this time Scripture implies that the antichrist breaks his agreement, invades Jerusalem and occupies their new facility, boasting that he is above God.

With this bold and daring move against Israel, the world will now witnesses the last years of the antichrist's ruthless authority. Micah contends his worldwide dominion will end only when he is confronted by the remaining members of the UN Security Council, the seven shepherds and eight principal men of Micah 5:5. A confrontation that culminates with the Battle of Armageddon as the final event before Christ's return. Micah records that fifteen men, having both military and political authority, are used by God to lead a war against the antichrist (and the false prophet).

Micah 5:
Vs. 5

> And this shall be the peace, when the Assyrian shall come into our land, and when he shall tread in our palaces. Then shall we raise against him seven shepherds and eight principal men.

Vs. 6

> And they shall waste the land of Assyria with the sword, and the land of Nimrod in the entrances thereof. Thus shall He [God] deliver us from the Assyrian when he cometh into our land, and when he treadeth within our borders.

Again, the previous events rest solely on New York's destruction as the financial capital of the world, a city that Scripture clearly states is also the capital of a world government order.

A Personal Vision

It may be difficult for some to grasp the full significance of what Revelation 18 is saying when it describes the downfall of Mystery Babylon as the financial capital of the world. However, what I am about to add to this study may offer some insight regarding the consequences of such a collapse.

I must first confess that I find it difficult to discuss or write about personal matters. This is especially true regarding the following vision, one that revealed something unpleasant which could happen to all of us. All too often listener and reader alike will tend to question one's credibility or emotional state. The result is a tendency for one to keep certain things to oneself for fear of being shunned or misunderstood. After years of reflection, however, I feel compelled to share just such an experience.

It began on a spring morning in 1971 as I was standing in my living room going over a large investment contract. It was a large document showing what would be available upon my retirement should I begin paying into it then.

And as I was reading its many pages and going over its contents. I found myself raised to the height of about a three-story church building and shown their enormous parking lot filled with people. I remember being impressed with how neatly dressed these people were, yet on all their faces were looks of terror and shock.

In the vision I was already aware of what had previously happened. The United States dollar had collapsed, and hundreds of people had lost all their financial security and did not know what to do or to whom they should turn. As I looked about the crowd, my eyes stopped at different people. And, in a fashion that I can best describe as resembling a strong zoom lens on a television camera at some sports event, four individual faces came before me from hundreds of yards back. Somehow I knew instantly what was on their minds and in their hearts.

On one face was a man angry with his union over the loss of his retirement funds. Another person was enraged at the government over the loss of her Social Security payments. And two others could not believe their investment companies and banks were bankrupt, leaving them totally without funds of any kind.

Then a voice said: "The reason these people are so terrified is because they have trusted more in the programs of man than in the Word of God, and

182

now they do not know what to do." Before I realized what had happened, I was again standing in my living room looking at the proposed investment contract. Being stunned at what I had just seen, I put the contract away to be examined later when I would be better able to concentrate on it.

It was about four days later that I decided to take care of that impending investment contract. And, going through the financial retirement portion, I again found myself above that same assembly of people and their painful expressions. Surprisingly I again knew what had happened to the U.S. dollar, and the same comment was heard regarding their fear and anger. Again, after seeing it exactly as in the first vision, I found myself looking at the investment contract. This time, however, I was even more confused and stunned than in the first incident four days earlier. And after folding up the investment contract, I filed it away for a later day.

Growing very cautious of picking up its contents, I waited for over a week to pass before I attempted to get back into this unfinished investment matter. As I began turning its pages to its promised cash benefits, I was again on the top of that same building looking down at the same horrified faces. Everything was repeated; however, after seeing the vision for the third time, I now was aware that the Lord had given me a brief look into the future, a financial collapse I was convinced that I would personally witness one day. I had never had a vision before the events of that spring, nor have I had one since, but I am certain that God had a purpose for giving me a glimpse into this nation's future.

Believing the Lord's return is near as proposed in this report, the Church, not aware of the dangers that are just ahead, could easily witness the monetary disintegration revealed in my visions. This financial collapse not only would open the door for the arrival of the antichrist, but would fulfill a host of other prophecies that the Church should be on guard for. Scriptural events that First Thessalonians warns begin as a thief's arrival in the dark of night:

Vs. 2

For yourselfs know perfectly that the day of the lord will come as a thief in the night.

Vs. 3

For when the world shall say, peace and safety, then sudden destruction cometh upon them, as travail upon a woman with child, and they shall not escape.

Vs. 4

But you brethren, are not in darkness, that day should overtake you as a thief.

Vs. 5

For we are the children of light, and of the day, we are not of the night, nor of darkness.

Vs. 6

Therefore, let us not sleep, as do others, but let us watch - and be sober-minded.

With the coming of the twentieth century, the Church has been given much to be concerned about regarding end-time prophecy, among them the birth of the nuclear age. Recent history has also added two additional ingredients for the Church to consider, and according to First Thessalonians, it is to do so very seriously.

These important events began with Israel being declared a nation again, followed by the rise of the oil-rich Arab States.

Scripture may also be telling the Church in the previous text that it should be especially aware of current events in the last days. And although not fully recognized on the surface as being important to prophecy, it would certainly include the recent 1990-91 Gulf War and the UN coalition in eliminating Iraq as aggressors in this area of the Middle-East.

Despite the coalition's fragile victory, and the world believing that it is again back on the avenue to global peace, Micah's fifth chapter states there will be additional problems ahead for all concerned regarding this matter of the Gulf war. This fact was made evident in the previous study of chapter five where Micah clearly identified the "Land of Nimrod" (Iraq) as the source of problems in the last days, and that the antichrist would come from this troublesome area.

Considering Iraq's defeat by UN forces Micah's prophecy should not be a total surprise. This is especially evident in light of the earlier study of the number "40", and how Scripture employed this number whenever any new or worthwhile spiritual event was about to take place. A prophetic number that also had a key role in braking Iraq's hold on Kuwait and ending the Gulf War. Military records reveal that it was in the early morning hours of January 16, 1992, that the invasion of Iraq by UN coalition forces (mainly U.S. Troops) began. The attack continued until Kuwait was liberated and fighting halted on February 25, making up a total of forty days and nights that may not only have launched the Church into a new period of prophesied events, but is, according to Saddam Hussein, "the mother of wars."

In addition to Iraq's humiliating defeat, the UN embargoes and inspections that followed could easily give Iraq cause for a nuclear attack against both the United States and the United Nations. Supporting this action is Daniel 7:24 and his comment that the antichrist is somehow responsible for the deaths of three horn members of the beast government.

This could be achieved should Iraq retaliate in some terrorist operation with one or more nuclear device against New York City. Such destruction would hit two birds with one (nuclear) stone, the U.S. Eagle and the United Nation's Dove. This crippling action to both the United States and the UN would quench some of Iraq's frustration over its recent defeat. It would also make Iraq out to be a hero within much of the Moslem world for successfully avenging itself against two of its most ardent enemies.

For a possible warning to the Church regarding the date of this world-shaking event, Scripture may be the most valuable source.

In Revelation 17:11, John records that a serious event is going to take place between the fifth and sixth kingdoms on a list of eight governments. Believing that this statement is directly related to his opening comment in verse one of this chapter, John implies that Mystery Babylon's destruction has something to do with the eight special kingdoms he referred to earlier as the "Inner Court".

Referring back to the chart on p.126, the list of the completed inner court now reveals that the destruction of Mystery Babylon takes place between the eagle/lion alliance and the bear.

In addition to Revelation's statement in verse 11 that the destruction of Mystery Babylon comes between the eagle/lion alliance and the government of the bear, Revelation 17:12, may have further pinpointed the time of Mystery Babylon's judgment. It states that the ten horns will serve the beast government for a term of **"one hour,"** which in terms of fractions, is equal to 1/24 of any given day.

Vs. 12
> **And the ten horns that thou sawest are ten kings [diplomats], which have received no kingdom as yet, but receive power as kings one hour with the beast [a seat on the S.C.].**

As previously examined, the actual term of the part-time members of the Security Council is two years under Article 23 of the UN Charter. As a result, the common denominator between the one hour (1/24) recorded in Scripture and the actual two years called for by the charter equates to 2/48 or 48 years when aligned with their two-year term. Consequently, by adding the number 48 to the year 1946, the date of the Security Council's first official meeting, the possible destruction of Mystery Babylon works out to be in the year 1994, or shortly thereafter.

While not wishing to discredit this study, this author fully recognizes the fact that this statement could prove to be absurd, especially when the same word in Revelation 18 is interpreted as being the brief period regarding the destruction of Mystery Babylon. Nonetheless, it may still be worth considering should Revelation's use of the term "one hour" be the key to identifying the date of this city's end. A term that would also help explain the angel's comment in the opening verses of Revelation 18, warning the Church to vacate this evil city.

As for the destruction of New York City, it could prove to be a spiritual blessing to the United States, that is greater then any financial hardship placed upon it. And in light of the prayers from within its churches regarding revival, this likelihood should not be a total surprise.

There are several instances of this probability recorded in the Old Testament. And like the many examples of correction regarding early Israel, the Scripture's reprimand to Mystery Babylon could also cause the United States to look again to God for moral direction. If then, this is that appointed generation, and the outcome is a spiritual renewal within the United States, should the Church not only prepare for such an event but applaud it as well?

Revelation 18:
Vs. 20

Rejoice over her [destruction], O heaven!
Rejoice, saints and apostles and prophets!
God has judged her for the way she treat-
ed you.

Vs. 21

Then a mighty angel picked up a boulder
the size of a large millstone, and threw it
into the sea, and said:

"With such violence the great city of
Babylon will be thrown down, never to be
found again." (NIV)

Notes